'I THOUGHT SOLIHULL WAS FOR SNOBS' (But These Punks Think Different)

THE MELL SQUARE MUSICK STORY

Punk/Mod Culture In '70s/'80s Solihull & Birmingham

Paul Panic

In memory of my dad Eric

And my mum Mavis

2

PAUL PANIC

'I THOUGHT SOLIHULL WAS FOR SNOBS' (But these punks think different)

The Mell Square Musick Story

Punk/Mod Culture In '70s/'80s

Solihull and Birmingham

Published by: - No Rip off Books in Association with 'Black Rose Ents'.

This being a book written in the true D.I.Y punk spirit, I make no apologies for bad grammar, slang, self indulgence, attitude, bad memory recall or lack of writing skills, it is written totally from the heart, read it, enjoy it, and then do something similar yourself, everyone has a story to tell!

The book title 'I thought Solihull was for Snobs' (but these punks think different) was originally spoken by David Coombs at the start of the Mell Square Musick E.P.   Paul Panic 2015

4

CONTENTS:

FOREWORD

With the passing of time it is perhaps inevitable that thoughts drift back to those carefree teenage years when anything seemed possible. I don't think I fully understood what a mortgage was, and life insurance, surely, was only for old people in case they died prematurely. Life however is short and before you know it, you've become the same age as you remember your parents being, when you were a teenager. I believe it's called; 'mid life crisis!'

Take a wander into any high street bookstore and you will see shelves full of celebrity, so called autobiographies, destined to reveal ultimately not a lot of truth, indeed often a lot of half truths and meaningless gossip. Therefore when writing this book I aimed to tell a true story of everyday characters who tried their best and in their own small way, each earned their own fifteen minutes of fame. Looking back a lot of the events in this book seem a lifetime ago but especially due to continued interest in the punk era and the ease of communication due to the internet, it constantly amazes me that I continue to get e-mails from all around the world asking for details about the records we released and informing me that our home made record is being played at for example, a barbeque in middle America or that a record collector in New Zealand knows who Paul Panic is!.

The fact that the band's music, mentioned in this book, is now available on Amazon and I Tunes, and that a DVD movie has been made of the story, as well as a double album of previously unreleased demo's being available worldwide, really is quite incredible! Many of the leading characters in the book are now scattered around the globe, living in countries such as Australia (Ed), Spain (Martin Hopeless), France (Sarah), Italy (Nick), Mexico (Dave Browne), Dubai (Tony), the United States (Mike Slamer and Chuck) and New Zealand (Mike Carter), but again due to the internet, it is easy to keep in touch and share the memories. Also the fact that almost all retain a keen interest in music and many still play and perform is testament to the good times we had when we were young.

It is heartening to go and watch young bands today, still full of ambition and fire just setting out on their musical journeys, not all will find success but each will surely have a wealth of stories to tell in the future, it's what music is best at – bringing people together to be creative, we may not in our case, have been supremely talented but we sure did have a lot of fun!!   **Paul Panic**

1/. ANTS

A childhood full of ants!! A strange way to remember my formative years, maybe, but my mother seemed to be fascinated by them, or rather their early deaths. She was often observed by the family, slipper in hand, examining floors and kitchen units, ready for the kill. Laying down powder trails around skirting boards and pouring boiling water down holes in the brick work. Maybe the summers were hotter then in the late 1960's, or maybe it was just our old house, but there always seemed to be ants sharing our living spaces.

I was born Paul Andrew Florence on June 3rd 1962 in Sorrento Maternity hospital in Moseley, Birmingham, the first child to my parents Eric and Mavis Florence, my dad worked as a sales representative for Plessey Telecommunications, my mum at that time was a housewife; Telstar by The Tornado's was the current number one in the singles chart celebrating the successful launch of the first communications satellite into space. Harold Macmillan was the Prime Minister and John F Kennedy the U.S President. Lawrence of Arabia was the most popular film at the cinema and sadly 130 people had died that day in an air crash at Paris Orly airport whilst taking off on an Air France flight bound for Atlanta Georgia.

It appeared I had a love of music from a very early age as when I was still a babe in arms, my mum would carry me, around the kitchen, dancing to the latest tunes on the radio. My aunt remembers some of my first words as being "Lika (sic) music mummy"

One of my earliest childhood memories was being in hospital at age four having had an eye operation, by this time I had a little sister Susan, born in June 1964. I can't remember the actual incident that led up to my operation very well, but apparently I had ran up to my mother who was in a telephone box at the time making a call, and tripped over the step and hit my head hard on the window of the box. I can clearly recall enjoying being in hospital, because each time my mum and dad came in, I got a new Dinky car or a new toy. My collection of Captain Scarlet and Joe 90 models grew by the day. I had the Joe 90 flying car and a shiny new red Spectrum Patrol Vehicle, over the next couple of days they were joined by the Spectrum Pursuit Vehicle and a model of an Angel Interceptor plane; Wow I liked this hospital malarkey!

I actually had quite a serious operation, as my right eye had been damaged and I was now to be the proud recipient of a small scar right in the middle of my forehead. It's still visible today.

I was also a proud member of the Tingha and Tucker Club with my orange and red fan club badge. This was a hugely popular children's television show in the sixties hosted by 'Auntie' Jean Morton; the club had a reputed 750,000 members at its height, and eventually had to close as they couldn't handle all the fan mail. I was also an avid viewer of 'Pogle's Wood' and 'Tales from the Riverbank' with Hammy Hamster as well as 'Camberwick Green', 'Trumpton' and 'The Woodentops'. By 1966 I was the proud owner of the 'Welcome to Camberwick Green' album on the Music for Pleasure label and indeed still own it, albeit now rather scratched, to this very day!

One of my favourite programmes when I was growing up was 'Casey Jones', watching his adventures on the Cannonball Express, was an early highlight in my life, I would sit transfixed for half an hour each week. Alan Hale Jnr played the legendary railroad engineer, and Dub Taylor, fireman Wallie Sims. Imagine my excitement when I found out that my dad had briefly worked as a fireman on steam trains too!

One of my earliest musical memories was at age six singing the 1968 hit 'Sunshine Girl' by Herman's Hermit's with my friends in the school playground, but altering the lyrics to make them a lot ruder. It was happening in schools all over the country of course, but to us it was very naughty indeed:

Sunshine girl, I'm looking down your bra,

I see two mountains; I wonder what they are,

Will you invite me, to squeeze them tightly?

Not bloody likely!

My sunshine girl

(Geoff Stephens/John Carter/Trad)

Little did I know back in those innocent childhood days that it was to be another song with the word 'bloody' in the verses that I would be associated with for years to come! But I am jumping ahead;

Our family lived in a semi-detached suburban area of Birmingham called Hall Green, totally unremarkable really except that I had to pass by Ann Haydon-Jones house on my way to school. Who is she? I hear you ask?, well Ann Haydon Jones was a very famous tennis star in the 60's, and legend has it that the Beatles themselves actually paused their dubbing session of 'Golden Slumbers' at E.M.I studio number 2 to listen to her live on radio, beat Billie Jean king for the Wimbledon title on 4th July 1969.

Sometimes I would take the long way home from school and pass by J.R.R. Tolkien's house, near Sarehole Mill, the very place he got his inspiration for writing parts of the 'Lord of The Rings' trilogy, or a few roads away where Tony Hancock the comedian had lived, I was living amongst the stars!

Early childhood memories are hazy, I had the obligatory imaginary friend who I had rather bizarrely named 'Sticky Sticky' and whose fantasy house I would always point out close to Hodge Hill Common, each time we went visiting my grandparents in Burton or Tamworth. Then on July 20th 1969 my mind comes into focus. Both me and my sister Susan, who was only five years old, and two years younger than me were put to bed earlier than usual, then woken up in the dead of night and brought downstairs. It was just before 4am when we witnessed possibly the greatest event in history. It was 'One small step for mankind'........and then back to bed for us. I can remember being so excited to be up at such a late hour and seeing grainy black and white pictures on our old monochrome television set in the corner. Men floating about in space, I remember it so clearly despite only being seven years old.

The family holidays usually were taken on the Norfolk Broads; we would descend en masse, the four of us, with added grandparents and aunts and uncles and assorted dogs, hiring ten berth boats and mooring up in Great Yarmouth or Lowestoft, Wroxham or near the notorious Potter Heigham Bridge, which was so low you had to engage the services of a pilot who would come aboard to guide your boat safely through, or if the tide was up, you wouldn't make it underneath at all. It was all such good fun being allowed to steer the boat along the waterways stopping at all the windmills and pubs on the way. My older cousins and uncles would be on the top of the boat sunbathing and drinking cans of 'Long Life' beer. Practical jokes were the order of the day, purchasing fake dog pooh and blaming the dogs, much to my Nan's disgust. She had a little Pekingese dog called Carla, and I can still hear her now saying to my dad, standing looking at a big plastic turd; 'my little Carla would never do that!'. We would go almost every year onto the Broads until some years later on when my dad bought a fixed caravan in Penbryn, west Wales. Actually he purchased it from Burton-on-Trent and it had to be driven down to Wales on the back of a low loader lorry, which as I remember was very tricky as the caravan was huge and the lanes very narrow. Many fun years were spent around that area of Wales visiting Llangrannog, Aberporth and Cardigan, all of them totally unspoilt, but being Wales the holidays often came with plenty of rain too, unfortunately.

One year we went to Butlin's Holiday Camp in Skegness, I was in heaven, and couldn't believe you could play on the fairground rides all day and it was free; amazing! Other times we would go for a day trip to Southport and ride the big wooden rollercoaster and play for hours in the Funhouse, riding the revolving barrel or trying to stay on the revolving disc. In those days you were allowed to take the car onto the beach and my dad used to let me have a go at driving, well steering at least. They were such happy carefree days.

1970 was the year that I became aware of the record charts and started wanting my own records, but it was to be another year before I bought my first single. I can however remember my sister Sue beating me to it, despite her being only six, asking my mum for a copy of the 'Pushbike Song' by The Mixtures which was on Top of The Pops and which we were now allowed to watch on Thursday evenings before bedtime.

1970 was also the first time I went to London; my parents took Sue and I down for a day trip to see the Tower of London, I can remember queuing up for what seemed like hours to see the Crown Jewels, then it was off to Madame Tussauds, where I was eager to get to the Chamber of Horrors and frighten my sister. Later we all sat watching the stars and planets in the London Planetarium, while my dad promptly fell fast asleep when they turned the lights out! I also seem to remember a visit to Battersea Funfair as well, to ride the Big Dipper. That was to close a few years later after a tragic accident when five children lost their lives caused by one of the trains detaching itself from the haulage rope. We would always be taken to the annual Christmas pantomimes, I remember seeing Jimmy Clitheroe and Mike Yarwood at Coventry Theatre at the age of six in 1968 , and other legends such as Freddie 'parrot face' Davies and Leslie Crowther. I was always fascinated by the purple binoculars between the seats that you put money into to release, my sister and I always took turns to use them for a better view of the stage.

Birthdays came and went but the one where I got given a mono 'Dansette' record player and an orange vinyl copy of 'Kumbaya' backed with 'Joshua fought the battle of Jericho' will stay in my memory for ever, I must have been only around 6 or 7 years old. Many times I was to be found armed with a hair brush microphone and tennis racket in front of the mirror miming along to that record. One day though, a year or so later I was playing in our large attic space and discovered a box of long forgotten 45 vinyl records belonging to my parents. Suddenly the joys of Rock' n 'Roll came into my life as I sorted through the hidden gems in the box. There were Beatles records; 'I feel fine' and 'She's a woman', and 'Day Tripper and 'We can Work it out', The Swinging Blue Jeans 'You're No Good' and 'Don't You Worry About Me', and Billy J Kramer and the Dakotas 'Trains and Boats And Planes' and 'little Children' .I soon asked my school friends to check what their parents had, and record playing sessions soon became a regular fixture after school at my house. I finally bought my first proper record at the age of 9 which was 'Funny Funny' by The Sweet, from a local record shop. Also at age nine in 1971, I heard a great record called 'Cousin Norman' by The Marmalade, which still remains a favourite, and was listening to 'Johnny Reggae' by the Piglets. Meanwhile Sue had bought 'Lady Rose' by Mungo Jerry.

18

By the age of ten I had made a lot of friends in our road and as we lived right opposite a country park called 'The Dingles', if we weren't to be found listening to records, we would be out exploring or fishing for sticklebacks in the river Cole. Around bonfire night we would go and buy boxes of Bronco Brand, red and green Bengal matches, and be amazed at the colours the flames produced. I remember often going to my friend Larry's house to listen to this amazing radiogram his parents owned. He seemed to have all the latest records, such as 'Poppa Joe' by The Sweet and 'Look wot you dun' by Slade as well as always playing the latest chart hits on the radio. By this time in 1972 The Marmalade had released another great single called 'Radancer' which had a great chugging guitar riff; it sounded really exciting to my ears at the time, and Neil Young had released 'Heart of Gold' which was just a fantastic record that I played all the time. At school though, the song that was a big secret for the boy's in the know was 'Big Six' by an artist called Judge Dread. Very few of my friends had actually heard it because the radio acted as if it did not exist, and put a blanket ban on any airplay, backed up by the cries of Mary Whitehouse who promptly had it banned. Strange, as it reached number eleven in the national charts; what was this all about? It became a record that was whispered about in the playground and therefore very exciting for young boys! My friend Larry somehow

19

managed to get a cassette of it and we all hurried round to his house after school to finally hear the tape. Very funny it proved to be too, with all the rude double meanings set to nursery rhyme reggae. Another fond memory of 1972 was a school assembly one morning taken by my music teacher Miss Cooper, she said triumphantly; number 16 in your hymn books and number 9 in the charts, 'morning has broken', a reference to the current hit song/hymn by Cat Stevens.

Another friend who lived a few doors away called Clive had a full size snooker table in a specially built shed at the bottom of his garden, that his dad had constructed, great days. I was only ten at the time but loved pop music, there was an older boy who lived further down the road who used to tell us it was all rubbish and that we should listen to the album he had bought by a rock group called 'Genesis', it was called 'Foxtrot'. I remember going round one day and thinking it was terrible, all really long songs with no catchy bits. I used to try and discover the new songs before my friends to impress them, and used to sit on the stairs at home to call up the Dial a Disc service, dialling 160 on the telephone to hear the Top 40 new releases; my parents were not too happy when the phone bill arrived I can tell you!.That was the first time I heard T.Rex's 'Telegram Sam' the rawness of the guitars really excited me. I used to get my mum to let me go into the local record store in Hall Green which was called Midland Music, they had a really high counter that I couldn't see over but my mum used to lift me up to read the Chart listings stuck onto the top and would buy me a 7" single most weeks before we went to do the weekly food shopping at Mac Fisheries supermarket, opposite.

Around this time during the winter of 1972/73 it was not uncommon for the house to be plunged suddenly into darkness during the evenings as a result of power cuts. The Miners were striking for fairer pay and the rest of the country was operating on a 3 or 4 day week. Out would come the candles and the torches, but I remember it all being immense fun and it certainly brought the family together and evoked a sort of wartime spirit amongst the neighbours, borrowing candles and swapping gossip.

The following year was 1973, which was a big year for me and for music in general, I had taken my 11-plus examinations at Hall Green Junior School which would determine if I was clever enough to go to Grammar School. My mum and dad were very keen to get me into King Edwards Grammar School in Birmingham as this was a prestigious school, but the word at my school was that all the 'posh' kids went there, so I wasn't keen at all. I passed the exams but not with high enough grades, so the next best choice was Moseley Grammar School. I then found out only 2 boys I knew from my old school were going there, so of course my parents invited them over for tea, their names were Chris Fallon and Alan Parkes. It was a huge boy's only school on the border of Hall Green and Moseley that looked like a cross between Hogwarts and a stately home. Actually, a really good school at the time, I remember being very impressed that they even had a film club at lunchtimes, although I only went twice, to see 'Billion Dollar Brain' and 'In the Heat of the Night'. They also did interesting subjects like Ancient history where we attended lectures and learnt all about Egypt and the pyramids. The worst part was that we had to play rugby; I hated it, all that mud and violence and sweaty jockstraps, so I used to cheat and add my name to the swimming rota whenever I could.

My interest in music prompted me to start learning the violin, which I assumed I would be able to master without too much bother, but in reality I was allowed to borrow the teacher's personal violin to take home one day and somehow it got returned with the addition of a crack in the wood of the body. This of course didn't go down very well at all with the teacher and resulted in a large bill for the repairs to my parents. Needless to say the violin lessons came to a somewhat premature end. This was the infamous school that was attended some years before by Chris Spedding, Bev Bevan, Frank Ifield and Jasper Carrott. While I was there everyone seemed to be into Jethro Tull, there was even a school band no doubt inspired by them called Josiah Wedgewood.

In the June of 1973 filming was taking place in Birmingham for the Cliff Richard film 'Take Me High'; I can remember my mum taking me and my sister Susan up to stand amongst the crowds in Corporation Street to watch as Cliff came up the street, sitting on the back of a sports car as part of a big street parade scene in the film. I remember we had waited with thousands of others for ages before anything happened, but it was a real carnival atmosphere. Years later I finally saw that film on video, and all the memories came flooding back.

Back in the real world though, glam rock had arrived with a vengeance, the guitars got louder and the fashions somewhat crazier, Slade were the number one band of the time, and it was great waiting for 'Top of the Pops' every Thursday to see what guitarist Dave Hill was going to wear. All the trendy lads at school were wearing star jumpers, a sort of woollen tank top with three stars sewn onto the front. Music became loud and brash and everyone's parents looked on in horror, especially when The Sweet appeared on the show, all dressed up wearing make-up, making them look like visitors from another planet. My mum at the time wasn't at all happy about some of the posters on my bedroom wall, those of The Sweet and David Bowie looking very androgynous in their feather boas and glitter. After that Slade were my parents preferred evil, as at least, by and large they vaguely looked like men!

We would wear 'Oxford bag' trousers as wide as possible with velvet pockets and platform shoes. I had a regular order of 'Popswop magazine', which I used to collect from the local newsagent's shop at the end of the road, along with my sister's copy of 'Mirabelle' or 'Jackie', and every fortnight I learnt more about rock music history from the 'Story of Pop' issues that were specially ordered for me. I was totally fascinated to learn about 50's rock'n'roll, skiffle, blues, and other types of music I had previously never heard of. I would also buy 'Disco 45' magazine that actually printed the lyrics to the chart hits of the day.

In 1974 my only real firm memory is going with my dad on a rare outing to see a film at the cinema, it must have been showing in the city centre, as we first had to catch a train from nearby Hall Green railway station. We spent a happy afternoon watching the just released Roger Moore film 'Gold'.

My mum would occasionally take my sister and I on weekend shopping trips to the Birmingham Bull Ring, which we always looked forward to as it meant we got to ride on the top deck of the bus and invariably got bought treats during the day. We would collect Green Shield stamps on her purchases, and along with the ones my dad got with his petrol, happily stick them in their collector books all evening, when we got home. It was always exciting to see the Rotunda and the 18ft tall statue of King Kong that stood in Manzoni gardens near the Bull Ring shopping centre. We would often walk along New Street and so it came as a huge shock on 21st November 1974 to learn that, allegedly the Provisional I.R.A, although they denied responsibility, had detonated two bombs killing 21 people, one in The Mulberry Bush Pub at the bottom of the Rotunda, and one in the Tavern in the Town in New Street. At the time this happened, many people were enjoying a night out watching a showing of the film 'Planet of the Apes' at Birmingham Odeon which was situated between the two pubs. Most of the dead were between the ages of 17 and 22, and a passing bus was also wrecked in the explosion. This was a huge shock and concern at the time and certainly made people think twice before entering the city centre for months to come, especially during the evening.

In 1975 at age twelve just two months before my thirteenth birthday, I announced to my shocked parents that I was going to see Slade play live at Birmingham Odeon, they of course said no, but somehow I talked them around after agreeing to let my dad pick me up afterwards. I actually went to this gig alone even though I was so young and was blown away by the sheer power of the band, I can still remember the show clearly and even the name of the rather lame support act, Bunny.

The Birmingham Odeon was always a great live venue and a well rehearsed game was played out each time a band played; you would get a cheaper ticket in the rear stalls and inch your way forward in the darkness and eventually outsmart the security by running to the standing area at the front of the stage, losing yourself in the crowd hoping not to be spotted. I bought a satin Slade scarf at that gig which stayed on my wall at home for quite some time afterwards.

When my parents sometimes went out in the evening with friends, an older girl from across the road Gillian used to come across and sit with me and Susan, she was into Cockney Rebel, that was when I first heard their album called 'Psychomodo' it left a huge impression on me, at the time, it just seemed such strange music with Steve Harley's unusual vocals.

2/. BUILDING FOR A BETTER FUTURE

Later in the year my parents decided to move house; records and all. I had never understood why my parents had bought such good records in the past but were now listening to Gracie Fields and Jack Jones, I guess their rock' n 'roll dream had expired somewhat. We were moving to live in Shirley, Solihull, where no one famous was from, although these days I suppose you could maybe include Richard Hammond from BBC's Top Gear or Simon Fowler from Ocean Colour Scene. I had to move my education to a local Comprehensive, simply called Lighthall School, which my mum was not too pleased about as it didn't have 'Grammar' in its name, but to me it sounded fine especially when I found out it was just around the corner from our house and I could easily come home for lunch if I wanted to.

But then I saw Solihull. Probably best described as the Knightsbridge of the West Midlands, at least it thinks it is! The sort of place where houses cost the earth, and to quote local comedian Jasper Carrott, "There's two cars on the drive, but sod all in the fridge"; parts of Solihull are shall we say 'very upmarket'. About a week after moving in, my mum found out that Phillip, a friend of mine from my Junior School in Hall Green had recently moved with his family too, and now lived just around the corner from our new house. An instant friend in a new land!, so we met up again and I was horrified, he'd become a different person, a real snob, not the same Phil I had known a year or so before at all, I quickly took note and started to size up my new environment.

I was still into all that glittered, Marc Bolan, Slade, Geordie, Hello, David Bowie, Sweet, Alice Cooper, even a leather clad Suzi Quatro had recently adorned my bedroom wall when I had found out that she shared my birthday. I had recently got myself a paper round to pay for my fast growing record collection. It wasn't long though, before I made new friends at my new school, Lighthall, and I settled into the new area quite happily. Around this time I discovered stereo sound, having been bought a 'Phillips' music centre, with a built in cassette deck. It suddenly meant I was able to record music directly from the radio and make up my own tape compilations that were always taken on any journeys we made as a family, and played loudly in the car, despite my mum and dad's constant pleas to turn the sound down.

My Parents, Eric and Mavis were born in Burton on Trent and Tamworth respectively, which meant all our family relatives lived quite a distance away from us, therefore I only got to see Cousins, aunts and uncles on birthdays and Christmas and the annual holiday to the Norfolk broads. Burton on Trent was/is a beer brewing town and my grandparents May and Fred used to run a pub, as well as some of my aunts and uncles too, but my dad had relocated first to Northampton then to Birmingham in search of work, before settling originally into the suburb of Hall Green.

Tamworth was perhaps most famous for its castle and the Reliant car factory but my mum first got a job at Doultons earthenware works in Wilnecote as an office clerk, before moving to work at Fort Dunlop in Birmingham, this proved exhausting with all the train travel to work, so she moved to Frank Spooner's Drapery shop on the Watling Street, back in Wilnecote. My mother when she was younger used to go dancing with Julian Cope's future father Alan, to the local Assembly rooms or parish hall dances held in Wilnecote, Tamworth or Dordon. She met and got engaged to a local man called Aubrey Turner, but he got conscripted into national service and had to move away. Eventually after the difficulties of trying to maintain a long distance relationship, she met my dad at another dance and broke off the previous engagement. My dad and his pals used to travel to Tamworth on the train from Burton-on-Trent and compete with each other to fix up dates for the following weekend, and then ride past the various dancehalls on the bus to see which girls had turned up. The dances were always on a Saturday evening and always finished at 11.45 sharp. In Tamworth the girls and guys would often walk what was called 'The Monkey Run', parading up and down the high street in the hope of getting noticed. The Pubs in those days were scary places for young people being full of old men and manual workers.

If you pulled a partner at the dance, chances are you would then arrange a date to go to either 'The Palace' or 'The Grand' cinema's during the week at one of their 6-8 or 8-10pm showings. It was at one of the dancehalls that my mum attended with her friend Irene, that she first met my dad and eventually relocated with him, after they got married, to live in Birmingham. My grandparents on my mum's side Eva and Ken lived in Wilnecote. I remember on our visits, my grandad always pressing a half a crown into my hand when we left and saying to me "Have a drink on me", and promptly shaking my hand off with his firm grip, he always did this but one week he seemed to have forgotten, and apparently I turned around bemused and was heard to mutter 'I will have a drink with you next time then

Grandad!'. Another favourite saying of his to me was "You should have had red hair".

My sister Susan when she was very small would wander into their front room and stare in wonderment, motionless, at the real fire not really understanding what it was. My grandad would spin dominoes on the table top and we would watch mesmerised. He had been a coal miner working down the local pit and had a miner's lamp on the mantelpiece. My Nan would make hot buttered scones and my aunt Doff (short for Dorothy), who hadn't married and still lived at home would always make a fuss of us, we loved it!

I often used to overhear my mum talking to her older sister Peggy on the telephone, relaying family news, and one day in late 1975, my mum told me that my older cousin Mike had been offered a record deal as he played in a band. They called themselves 'Back in the Band'. But the deal specified they must find a new band name; they soon changed it to City Boy. I then found out they were due to play at a Birmingham night-club called 'Barbarella's but despite my appeals I was told I was far too young to go as it was strictly over 18's only.

By this time I was avidly watching music on the television but the BBC's, Top of the Pops was full of really weak sounding pop bands, it was like trying to find loud guitars in a haystack, the music scene had gone really stale, with no excitement at all. There just wasn't anything interesting to buy anymore, most of the glam bands had gone quiet, and I found myself checking out bands like Genesis again and even Kiss, simply because their record covers looked interesting, the music on the inside certainly wasn't to my taste most of the time. I was aching for something loud and fast and although it sounds crazy now, songs like 'New York Groove' by Hello had to suffice, even Slade were doing ballads like 'In For A Penny' at the time, believe me 'Wild Thing' by The Goodies was about as wild as it got for a while! Where was the loud guitar attack of songs like 'Hellraiser', or 'Cum on feel The Noize'.

I abandoned the search for a while and got into the new craze of skateboarding, I made some new friends at school; there was David 'Wally' White, David Coombs, Trevor Hughes, Laurence Jones and Keith Hobbs, we all used to dare each other to find steeper and steeper hills to skate down, this was our new way of finding some thrills I suppose, as previously we used to make go-carts out of old pram wheels and bits of wood and have races around the block and across the local allotments.

My dad was a sales rep for a telecommunications company at the time, I can remember him bringing home many of the spoof chain letters that got passed around his office, the sort that now would be considered very un politically correct but one day he came home with a glossy brochure from a Skateboard Company based in Solihull called 'Morris Vulcan'. It wasn't long before I had a great board but this was in the days of solid wheels and hard wooden decks, and one day I was skating down a steep hill into an alleyway between some houses, I crouched down on the board to duck under one of those barriers that stopped people riding bikes through, hit a stone on the floor that stopped the board dead and came off at speed ending up in hospital with my leg broken in 2 different place's. At the time I was with my friend, Laurence, who ran off to get his mother when he saw what had happened and she arrived in her Mini car to rush me to hospital. I remember being in such pain, and being unable to bend my leg to get in. Eventually I was manoeuvred onto the back seat in agony, and ended up in hospital suspended in traction. I was well and truly plastered for the rest of the year.

My parents told me that my cousin Mike's band, that were now officially called City Boy, were going to be supporting the Irish band Thin Lizzy at Birmingham Town Hall in October, but as I had my leg in plaster they didn't think I should go. Needless to say I went anyway with my aunt Doff, crutches and all, and very nearly got crushed back into hospital. That night I think I saw the light, City Boy were a revelation live, with the local crowd solidly behind them, and this was my cousin! As for Thin Lizzy all I can say is they instantly became my favourite band, I had never heard anyone so loud. I very quickly went out and bought the 'Rosalie' single. The following year 1976, Thin Lizzy became massive with their 'The Boys are Back in Town' and 'Jailbreak' records. The later was the first 7" I had ever owned in a picture sleeve. Although the singles were great, their B-sides, were all long guitar solos, I felt a bit cheated, but didn't really understand why.

This band thing however was interesting me more and more, and then one day one of the so called 'posh kids' at my new school announced to whoever would listen that he was in a band now as well. They were called 'Las Vegas' and they were to play at the 'end of term review concert' in the school hall, but not until they had rehearsed a set of songs, it would be a whole year later that they finally did play at the end of term review show. This was in June 1977.

Meanwhile 1976 was pretty much the same as 1975 in Solihull, paper rounds to finance my ever growing singles collection, discovering girls existed (Tina and Della where are you now?), and the biggest shock was discovering some of the others at school had record collections too. The kids at Lighthall School fell into two distinct musical camps, the swots were always into the so called intellectual sounds of Genesis, Pink Floyd, Uriah Heep, and Jethro Tull, but some others I found out, loved the so called noisier guitar based music I liked too. There was Colin Abrahall, David White, Martin Hope, and Laurence Jones to name just a few. Had they all stolen my music taste? 'NO!', these were brothers in arms, birds of a feather, hallelujah!!

At the time the most popular British soap opera on television was 'Crossroads', the life and times and everyday goings on at a fictional motel in a made up suburb of Birmingham called 'Kings Oak', it was on every week day at teatime when I got home from school. My mum was always a big fan, there was a popular character in the show called Miss Diane (played by actress Sue Hanson, who was in real life married to Carl Wayne lead singer of The Move), she was married in the show to a postman called Vince Parker, but eventually they went their separate ways. Imagine our surprise at school when shortly afterwards we were introduced to our new French teacher, yes it was the man himself, Vince Parker (real name Peter Brooks), he only stayed for one term as I remember, as all the kids used to rib him constantly about 'Miss Diane', and call out

"Vince" all the time in lessons. It was a real shock when he first walked into that classroom; perhaps he thought no one would recognise him, very funny though.

During the long summer break in 1976 our young minds were working overtime, plotting and planning, but of course we had very little money, still being at school, so any thoughts of forming bands had to wait. By the time the school holidays were over, and we had all returned to school in September, rumours began to circulate at school about a club in the city centre called 'Barbarella's, apparently putting on some interesting new bands, someone claimed to have been at the gig AC/DC played there in July, but we found out he had been lying to us and he eventually admitted it was his elder brother who went. Still we were very impressed as they were a very noisy anti-social type of band from Australia, and the tape of their 'High Voltage' album was being passed around the school, we, still being schoolboys ourselves, thought it was very funny that the guitarist was dressed as a schoolboy on the cover, and that it contained a track called 'Can I Sit Next To You Girl' which seemed very naughty and suggestive at the time, I used to go home and sit in my favourite place on the top of my wardrobe and listen to all those songs with the volume turned up to the max.

3/. CATCHING THE BUZZ, 1977 YEAR ZERO

Something was stirring in London clubs throughout the summer of 1976, with a new kind of music the press later called 'Punk Rock', but although at the time we didn't really know much about this, we had noticed bands with strange names starting to appear in the gig listings in the back of the three weekly music papers 'Sounds', 'New Musical Express', and 'Melody Maker'. There was a Birmingham band called Suburban Studs who had played at 'Barbs' as we now called it, supported by a new band from London called The Clash, this was October 27th 1976, but again no one we knew had been present.

Then each time we ventured into Birmingham we would see posters in record shops and pasted on walls advertising bands with great names like The Killjoys, Ha Ha Germs, Dum Dum Boyz, Dansette Damage, Model Mania, and The Clerks. It was all to do with this Punk thing that was happening in London, with some band called the Sex Pistols.

At this time no-one in our year at school had been to Barbarella's simply because we were too young to be allowed in. It had to be worth learning more though, as this was the same club my cousin's band had already played at the year before. It all sounded really exciting, it seemed like we were missing out on something really big happening.

You know what it's like at school, mention something new you want to find out about, and suddenly people you have never spoke to before profess to suddenly know it all.

Jeremy was a friend of a friend and one day mentioned that his elder brother had a bass guitar for sale for five pounds. Hang on though, surely electric guitars cost hundreds of pounds didn't they? According to Jeremy, it was perfect and even had a case, so without even a thought of how to play the thing, and a week's paper round money in my pocket, I and my friend David Coombs, went to inspect the legendary beast one lunchtime. Then the truth came out, he had a bass guitar, that much was true, but it had no strings, no electrics, pick-ups, or metal of any description on it, just a guitar shaped piece of wood. It was really heavy man! It seemed to weigh a ton. So of course I had to buy it, I then sprayed it shiny gold and spent many a five minutes posing in front of the mirror pretending to be Phil Lynott, thinking this will be easy to get working once I buy some strings. It wasn't long before the novelty wore off and it was abandoned in the garden shed.

One Sunday, I know it was a Sunday because the bag was extra heavy with all the big thick Sunday papers, I was slogging along doing my recently acquired paper round, when tired, I stopped for a break and started leafing through someone's copy of 'News of the World'. I was amazed to see a piece about that London band the Sex Pistols and a so called anti-social record they had released called 'Anarchy in the U.K'. I knew instantly I had to have it, even without having heard it, I knew it would be great. It was however, like the search for the Holy Grail, trying to find that record in our neighbourhood. Eliciting responses such as "Never heard of it mate", or "Oh it's been withdrawn for being obscene, we never stocked it". It was quite a while later that I finally got to hear it. It had become for a short while, a mythical beast of a record to me and my friends, but we did start listening to the other small amount of punk rock that was around.

John Peel, the Radio One late night D.J could always be relied on to be the first to give airplay nationally to any new interesting bands, and by the time I had discovered his 10pm-midnight show, lying listening in bed every night with my headphones on, he was already starting to play punk records in between the usual Reggae, Status Quo, and progressive rock favourites. I heard my first ever punk singles like 'New Rose' by The Damned, 'Blitzkrieg Bop' by The Ramones, and 'Live at the Marquee' by Eddie and the Hot Rods .That was it for me, I realised the kind of music I had longed to hear all along was now coming out thick and fast by lots of new bands I had previously never heard of. It's strange looking back because there really was a need for this kind of music and attitude at the time, everything previously on radio had sounded so safe and watered down, that's why the small bits of loud guitar we did hear in the charts, songs like 'Rock' n' Me' by Steve Miller Band, or 'Standing in the road' by Blackfoot Sue were so important, it just needed to be faster and with more attitude, and now suddenly it was as if everyone had woken up and done something about it, all at the same time. Therefore all the band names, the more outrageous the better, started appearing on my school army green rucksack in marker pen, as well as on the cover of my maths book, much to the disgust of the teachers! Who on earth were the Stranglers?

During 1977 the tabloid papers were full of the usual shock stories associated with anything deemed anti-social by the establishment, and so suddenly it was 'Punks battling Teddy Boys in London's Kings Road', the press seemed to revel in the comparisons with the sixties fights in British seaside towns between the Mod's and the Rockers. Predominantly this seemed to be a London thing, nothing much like it was happening in Birmingham at the time.

The music though was certainly not a hype, the records were appearing every week, and I very quickly had to rely on making 'wants' lists of titles scribbled down as fast as John Peel could play them. I couldn't afford to buy all these records but as long as I stayed in touch and knew what was available I was happy. That list, growing each day was soon to be my music reference bible.

The story of punk rock in 1977 has been well documented elsewhere, the razor attacks on Johnny Rotten, the Sex Pistols on the Bill Grundy Show, the Jubilee boat trip, the rise of The Clash, Damned, and Buzzcocks, but the year's best moment for me came on March 17th, when off I went alone again, because my mates allegedly couldn't afford it, back to the Birmingham Odeon, but this time to see a punk band for the very first time live. The concert was to be T. Rex supported by The Damned, what a night that was, they just didn't care, the bass player Captain Sensible was dressed up as a nurse, there appeared to be a vampire on lead vocals and a guitarist and drummer who played like there wasn't going to be a tomorrow. Two of the band even reappeared to play with Marc Bolan at the end of his set on 'Get it On' It was an epiphany for me, and from that night onwards I knew it was time to form a band of my own. I couldn't play anything, but so what, what did that matter anyway? Marc Bolan was, and still lives on immortally as the 'Prettiest star', I had all the T. Rex singles, and despite Glam Rock being everything Punk professed not to be, the combination of the two bands worked well, simply because Marc was honest and open to new styles and trends and not afraid to let The Damned support him. He had his own television series at the time called simply 'Marc' which saw a few punk bands getting valuable television exposure, bands such as Generation X, Radio Stars and the Boomtown Rats.

4/. DAMNED, NEW ROSES AND ZITS

Between the ages of ten and fourteen, it had become the Christmas time ritual in our house for me and my sister Sue to entertain the relatives with a little show, the lights would be turned off and by the light of the Christmas tree in the corner, we would both descend the stairs, with tennis rackets round our necks to replicate guitars, wearing tinsel covered clothes. All our aunts and uncles and grandparents would applaud loudly, as we would mime along to 2 or 3 songs blasting out from the music centre in the corner. It was my first taste of performing to an audience. I loved it and took it very seriously carefully selecting the music each year. We performed to 'Blockbuster' by The Sweet, with Sue having practised the bit which went 'I just haven't got a clue what to do' perfectly in time, and covered in make-up just like the bands bass player Steve Priest. Our favourite song though was always 'Where have all the good times gone' the David Bowie version of the classic Kinks song from his album 'Pin-Ups'. As an encore we used to do 'My Ding a ling' by Chuck Berry, complete with all the innuendos, which the adults no doubt understood better than we did at the time. It was a rehearsal of sorts for what was to come.

Meanwhile back at school, my teachers must have appreciated my graffiti covered maths book, because I was moved up a class, and became good friends with Martin Hope and Ian Colley who sat behind me at the back of the class. Ian lent me the first album by 999, another London based punk band, and before long, talk of forming a band of our own took over from the algebra and fractions. The school review was coming up at the end of term and that long awaited appearance of Las Vegas the school rock band. When the day finally came, we all waited patiently in a packed school hall, the curtain went up and there they were, looking and sounding like the last year hadn't happened, all eyes to the fret-boards, and incredibly tame. I can remember them playing a couple of Beatles songs, 'I Saw Her Standing There' was one I think, but what a disappointment, this wasn't Punk Rock at all!, but looking back at least they got up there and tried, it was just a shame things had moved on. Then just as if to emphasis the point, the next act was two of the more attractive girls in the school (Tina Cappuccitti and Della Field), with their hair in pigtails and skirts hitched up, wearing lots of black eyeliner and pogo dancing to 'Go Buddy Go' by the Stranglers, they got the whole hall up dancing and shouting, that was the moment punk rock had finally arrived at Lighthall School. It was now time for the long summer break, and talk of forming a band was a serious consideration, even if it took a little while longer for that talk to become a reality.

It was announced in the music press that a big punk festival called 'Britain's Burning' (a reference to The Clash song 'London's Burning') was to take place at Birmingham's Rag Market on July 17th 1977. The Rag Market was a huge market hall sited behind the Bull Ring Shopping Centre and it looked like it would make a fantastic venue for band's to play in. The line up of bands was impressive, it was to be headlined by The Clash, with Australian punk band The Saints, American's Cherry Vanilla and Snatch, French band Stinky Toy's, and from England, Subway Sect, Shagnasty, and The Slits. There was a full page advert in 'New Musical Express' and Martin and I made eager plans to attend, then the local council got nervous about the event after a complaint from the Vicar at the church opposite the market and it was cancelled on the very day it was to take place. The Clash and Shagnasty turned up and eventually they were able to borrow some equipment from local heavy metal band Warhead and put the word out to all the loitering punks that they would play later that night at 'Barbarella's'. Sadly we didn't make it. A month or so later on August 16th, the news came through that Elvis Presley had died, but to us at that time it just signalled the end of the old style of music, all we wanted to listen to was punk and the new wave.

Barbarella's club then set up its own mini punk festival on bank holiday Monday August 29th, featuring a whole day's worth of bands such as Eater, The Drones, and bands from Birmingham such as Model Mania, The Killjoys, Rudi and the Rationals and Spizz Oil. Oh how we longed to go to that one too, but again the problem of being underage and not being allowed into a nightclub put the blockers on the idea for us yet again.

So the holidays came and went, then just after starting the new term on September 17th I awoke to the news that Marc Bolan was dead, I remember my mum came into my room while I was still in bed and told me, and at first I thought she must have heard it wrong. I couldn't believe it. I had only seen him live a few months earlier, I felt really upset and emotional, and it just wasn't fair!

Angry music to express my feelings became all the more important, this world was insane!

Jasper Carrott the local Birmingham comic who had a somewhat unexpected hit single with 'Funky Moped' which reached number 5 in the U.K charts back in 1975 (although a lot of the sales were due to its B-side which was a rather risqué spoof script for the children's television programme 'Magic Roundabout'), had introduced the word 'Zit' into common usage in the English language, as a slang word for a spot, or pimple, although apparently widely used in the United States, it was largely unheard of in Britain at the time.

Martin Hope had actually got a band started during the summer break and called it The Zits, I didn't find out about this until we started back at school in September. None of the members could play their instruments properly, but because his dad was involved in the running of the Shirley Pipe and Drum Band, they had access to a rehearsal room at the local Scout Headquarters. Luckily for the residents of Shirley, the Scout Hut was well away from any houses, the noise must have been horrendous.

All those months of rock n roll dreaming when in our early teens were fun, but now here was Martin actually in a real band, someone my age, with the same lack of talent as me, actually beginning to live the dream. This was now looking like a serious situation. I mean, what if he had to leave school before the exams to be a star? I was well aware that the punk band Eater had a drummer named 'Dee Generate' who was only fourteen and they already had a record out called 'Outside View'. This was really serious in my mind! But then I actually heard The Zits, first at a rehearsal, then later at an actual gig they had set up for the venture scouts and their mums and dads at the headquarters, very punk rock I remember thinking at the time!.

The Zits consisted of Martin Hope(less) on a 'Kay' guitar, purchased for twenty four pounds, Neil (Nelly the nose) Collins on drums, Richard 'Billy' Baker on bass guitar and Michael Carter on guitar. The lasting memory of their one and only gig is of a band with no rhythm at all, the drummer played in the Pipe and Drum band, but didn't know about drum kits so just played the tom toms (there was no beat at all!, the guitarist Mike looked painfully shy, and just stood still most of the time looking embarrassed. Mike Carter now lives in New Zealand but has some memories of his own:

"I learnt to play six string acoustic guitar aged 8, playing and singing folk songs such as 'Puff the Magic Dragon' or the 'Streets of Durham Town'. I had lost interest by aged 10 and to be honest I was never very good, even my parents encouraged me to give it up. I started to get

interested in music again in my early teens and in 1977 aged 14, I started listening to some punk and got acquainted with the John Peel Show. My favourite band from the punk era was Stiff Little Fingers. John played the whole of the first album 'Inflammable Material' back to back. I first saw them when they supported the Jam at the Odeon in Birmingham they were awesome and I followed them avidly for a few years".

"Alongside the interest in punk, I also picked up a new hobby in electronics, and in particular sound systems. The two went nicely together and when the concept of forming a punk band was floated, it was in the technology side of things that my interest was first sparked. Picking up an electric guitar for the first time and getting it going through a big amp was a buzz, I soon realised that learning to play again would have its rewards. After all, half a dozen chords were enough - how hard could it be?"

"So the Zits were formed, using the Scout hut as our practice venue and the scouts audio gear for a P.A. (Martin's old man had the key for the cupboard!). I had to modify a couple of microphone input boards to suit the guitars. We borrowed a couple of six string guitars from mates and our drum kit consisted of a tenor drum and snare from the Scottish Bagpipe band based at the scout hut, and a single cymbal fitted to a homemade stand. The four of us were Martin 'Punk' Hope (lead vocals), Neil Collins (drums), Bill Baker (guitar) and Mike Carter (guitar) and backing shouting. We started off playing cover versions of The Clash and The Sex Pistols but to be honest they were so bad we figured to avoid comparisons; we were better off playing original material. Martin 'Punk' Hope was the main writer, coming up with such great songs such as 'I Pay my Rates', based on the comments of one of the scout leaders when he realised one of our number was stealing paper from the council offices on a regular basis".

"The short life of the band culminated with a single gig in the scout hall to an audience of about 25 astonished and pretty shocked venture scouts, leaders and a few other mates. We were dreadful but passionate, and very loud".

"Martin went on to join The Accused and I helped them out a couple of times with technical stuff. My time with The Zits was short but very memorable. I guess if The Accused had made it big I'd be feeling like Pete Best did about the Beatles!"

Mike Carter – The Zits

The audience just looked on blankly at that one and only gig by The Zits and didn't know what to say or do, I remember the scouts throwing paper aeroplanes at the band as they shouted and banged their way through the set. I was still really jealous because all I had was a bass guitar with no strings or electrics, rotting away in the garden shed.

I then started to hang around with Martin more and used to help carry their small amount of equipment to the rehearsals, actually it all looked really good, even a proper stage to play on, it was just that when they actually tried to

51

play it became unbearable. At the next rehearsal after the gig I was watching as usual, and just couldn't keep quiet any longer, so I walked up onto the stage and told Billy who was by now singing, and who I didn't really know at all, that I would show him how to do it properly, and promptly grabbed the microphone and proceeded in my best Johnny Rotten tone to shout my way through their song 'Cancer Research', oh dear, what was I doing? I couldn't sing either!, but I did know how to put on a show. It was goodbye Billy; I never saw him again after he walked out in a huff. Unfortunately what I hadn't bargained for was that Martin told me a few days later that the band had split up, apparently Neil the drummer was Billy's best friend and well it wasn't fair on him was it? It turned out that Martin and the guitarist Mike, had recorded a demo tape before the bands demise in Martins front room at home, which meant all the classics such as 'Mummy wouldn't let me', 'I pay my rates', 'Cancer Research' (doing a good job), 'You Prat', 'Politics' and 'Exploitation' were preserved for posterity, but definitely under lock and key. Martin told me he was going to see The Jam supported by The New Hearts at the Top Rank in Birmingham on November 28th, but I couldn't afford it.

As 1978 arrived and studies for exams took over, the idea for forming a new band was put on hold for a few months, but we still found time to start writing songs. We were now fast approaching sixteen years old, and being red blooded males we found out that The Rezillos led by Fay Fife, who we had seen in 'Sounds' music paper wearing micro mini-skirts and tight tops were going to be playing at 'Barbarella's'. We knew instantly we had to finally go and find out for ourselves what this punk club was all about. 'Mummy,   can   I   go? ....EH!... ------- 'NO!!!' well I'm going anyway, I will find a way to get in this time, never mind being two years too young. It was the first time any of us had ever been to a nightclub, but we were going and no one was going to stop us this time.

5/. EH! MUMMY WOULDN'T LET ME – SO WHAT!

Martin and I stood in the queue outside Barbarella's, which was located in Cumberland Street, Birmingham, almost opposite the Crescent Theatre, it was 9 o'clock, pm, we were 2 years underage, wearing torn up clothes that we had customised ourselves, fake birth dates fully rehearsed in our minds. We need not have bothered; we walked straight in past the door staff, without any trouble at all.

Quite a few songs have been written about Barbarella's over the years, but my favourite has to be 'Barbarella's' by The Prefects, one of the city's first punk bands formed by Robert Lloyd who later was in The Nightingales, and who ran Vindaloo Records. The Lyrics to that song sum the club up nicely:

'Barbarella's, Barbarella's, they got toilets, they got ashtrays, Barbarella's'. (Robert Lloyd)

What a great club, it was dark, slightly 'seedy', everyone was dressed to impress, it was owned by Birmingham's king of clubs, Eddie Fewtrell, who also had a number of other clubs in the city such as 'The Cedar Club', and 'Rebecca's'. There have been other songs about the club released since too, namely 'Barbarella's' by The Photo's and 'Barbarella's' by Stephen Duffy, they are all different songs despite having the same title. The club was located in Cumberland Street, just off Broad Street, which is now the city's main Entertainment area. You would pay your £2.50 admission and enter into a long dark corridor with a cloakroom on the right and toilets further down. It was swathed in dark red lighting and displayed framed pictures on the wall of cabaret artists from the club's past. There always seemed to be locked doors everywhere; one such room was rumoured to be a roller disco, but it always seemed to be closed. The rooms all had strange names such as 'The Pose', 'The Spectrum' and 'The Sin Bin'. At the end of the dark red corridor was the venue itself, with a raised area to the right with tables and chairs on, and a D.J booth to the left of the stage that usually played dub reggae, and a few punk tracks when the records became available, (echoes of Don Letts at The Roxy Club in London's Covent Garden).The venue itself was able to hold a few hundred people but when it was full you had to be prepared to get squashed and very sweaty. The stage was raised at the end of the room and was a typical small club size, complete with glittery cabaret style drapes along the back wall, and a hatch and ladder, that led up to the dressing room above the stage, therefore enabling bands and artists to appear on stage unseen by the crowd. To the right of the stage was a recessed area, with a post office style queuing system; this was the burger bar selling hamburgers, hot dogs, chips etc, served in little baskets, I can almost smell the fried onions now. What a great idea, beer and burgers in a night club. The bar was up a few steps at the back of the room opposite the entrance corridor, and was tiny, but if you were patient you could get yourself a pint of lager for 40 pence and then probably get it knocked out of your hands by pogoing punks on your way back through the crowd.

I remember once standing behind Captain Sensible from the Damned in the burger bar queue (he must have been just having chips of course, as he is a vegetarian!), with him talking about how he loved playing at Barbarella's as you didn't have to go out to find hot food, these days I know he is a fan of another 'Brummie' legend in fast food, 'Mr Egg', but that's another story!.To the right of the burger bar was another, always closed room, where they had disco nights at other times in the week.

Everyone at The Rezillos gig seemed to have a leather jacket on except us, and we were fascinated by the band names sprayed on the backs of them, most of which we were proud to say we had heard of now. One of the things that surprised us both was that despite some punks looking odd and a bit scary, everyone was really friendly, selling fanzines, and discussing all the latest bands.

The first group on was a new band I didn't think I knew called Gang of Four, but when they played 'Damaged Goods', I remembered having heard them on the John Peel show. The place exploded, with a mad rush to the front of the stage, and everyone jumping up and down. We stared in awe at a crazy guitarist playing the most disjointed manic riffs, and at the end of their set they were joined on stage by Fay Fife to perform 'I Can't Stand My Baby'. The Rezillos came on stage at around 11.45pm to the intro music from Thunderbirds, and everyone went berserk. The energy was amazing and they played some really great songs from their first album imaginatively entitled 'Can't stand the rezillo's. After two encores they had to leave the stage as guitarist Luke Warm a.k.a Jo Callis cut his hand.

I had heard about pogoing, but this was just crazy, the whole crowd, swaying, spitting, falling down in packs, were invading the stage at every opportunity. The band were cartoon characters of joy playing their songs 'Flying Saucer Attack', 'My Baby Does (Good Sculptures)', and 'Somebody's Gonna Get Their Head Kicked In Tonight', one anthem after another, but a lot of people were spitting at the band?, surely that wasn't right?, but in those days nobody seemed to care. If only my parents could see me now, diving around, T-shirt ripped to shreds, covered in sweat, beer, and spit, and yet it all felt so right. I thought of my sister Sue, at home asleep with her Starsky and Hutch posters and David Cassidy records, and realised she would need to be re-educated! I looked around and saw Martin standing at the bar looking like a scarecrow but with a huge smile all over his face.

'Oasis' in Birmingham was and still remains a multi level store that pretends to be a market. It is full of small units incorporating a number of fashion designers, record stalls and hairdressers. In later years, both Boy George, and Martin Degville of Sigue Sigue Sputnik, would both run stalls in there. One little unit in the basement sold bondage trousers, P.V.C shirts, and all the designer punk gear that we hated, but one day I noticed they had a Sex Pistols L.P on the wall called 'Spunk'. I couldn't believe it; I didn't think that they had released an album yet. It was then that I discovered what bootlegs were.

The following week they were stocking another one by the Sex Pistols called 'Indecent Exposure' with a really professional sleeve, which Martin bought for twelve pounds, a small fortune in those days. We finally got to hear what this almost mythical band sounded like, and for weeks afterwards that record never left the turntable.

It wasn't long before we started going to Barb's every week, no matter who was playing, it became our place, and certainly the place to be seen. There didn't seem to be any punk bands from Solihull apart from a local character called 'Spizz' who just used to turn up and jump on stage in between the bands with his sidekick Pete Petrol, to become the uninvited support band, he often got away with it, but at other times was heckled off by the crowd. There was a rumour that another band existed in Solihull called Swell Maps, but they never seemed to gig locally, and seemed to be a bit arty, but by July 1977 they had recorded the classic 'Read about Seymour' to be released by Rough Trade Records in London. We couldn't believe it, here was a band 'Punk' in spirit, even if not totally in sound, they had about as much talent as us. They only lived a few roads away from us and they were making a record for Rough Trade, the most happening record label and shop in London. It was time to up our game and actually do something about it.

Around the same time in that summer of '78 another school friend of ours, Colin Abrahall, had started a band with his friends Andy, Jock, and Sean, We had been on a Geography Field Trip, the previous year, lasting a week, to the school's cottage in Wales and Colin had been instrumental in dividing all the kids into Squaddies or Commando's on the coach down there, to play pranks. When we arrived the teachers had a real tough time, with all the covert raids we used to launch on their rooms, to put toothpaste in their slippers or causing minor avalanches down the valleys, aiming to narrowly miss them with rocks. The only work we seemed to do was throwing oranges into the river, to follow them down stream, 'did I say work?'

Colin lived not far from me, and used to have hair in long blonde spikes, I can remember my mum being horrified at his appearance as he passed by our house each morning on his way to school. I of course thought he looked great and used to experiment with my own hair, but mine just didn't seem to want to stick up, just as well really as it would probably been too much for my mum at the time. Actually my parents were really surprisingly liberal, and even allowed me to have a graffiti wall in my bedroom that my friends used to spray-paint band logo's on. My friend Lorraine would love to put David Bowie lyrics up there as well. "A crack in the sky and a hand reaching down to me" ('Oh you pretty things' David Bowie)

The band Colin had started that last term at school was called 'Charged G.B.H', who 36 years later are now internationally known. They all started regularly drinking at 'The Crown', which is a pub at the back of New Street railway station in the city centre. By the time of Punk's second wave of band's in '80/'81 it had become the drinking place of choice for Birmingham's Punks.

In 1980 G.B.H recorded their first demo tapes and the rest is history. When we finally heard their first released 12" single in 1981 'Leather, Studs, Bristles, and Acne', Martin and I looked at each other and thought we may as well give up, as it was as 'punk' as you could get, loud, very fast and simply on fire. It was like there were now two totally different punk styles, the class of '77, and the new bands that played at breakneck pace. The Crown produced other Birmingham punk legends such as the Velvet Underpants (the best comedy punk band ever), Drongoes for Europe, P.P and the Pungent Smells, Dead Wretched and The Sadists to name just a few.

6/. FINALLY VICTIMIZED IN 1978

During one of our regular Friday nights out at Barb's, I think it was at a gig by The Lurkers, Martin and I formed The Victims. We had no musical ability, which we actually saw as a major advantage. I chose the easy job of becoming the singer, Martin was to be on guitar, Ian Colley on Bass, and Laurence Jones on drums (well actually he had only one snare drum at this stage). I only remember us having one real get together, which was a band meeting at Laurence's house, or to be more precise we just met in his dad's garage and talked about ideas for the band. This soon degenerated into a drinking party of sorts, with bottles of cider and his parent's homemade wine. Ian drank so much that upon trying to stumble home, he became somewhat disorderly, which in turn lead to some local residents calling the police; when they arrived he promptly bit the officer's hand and passed out in the gutter. Next thing we knew he was being carried into an ambulance. He was taken to Solihull Hospital where he had to have his stomach pumped; He really was a Victim, although back at home the next day he claimed not to remember a thing!

Our previously appointed drummer had been a school friend David White, who was very keen but didn't have any drums, so he quickly left, we actually wrote a song about him entitled 'Dedicated,' the chorus was: "Used to have a drummer Wally White, left The Victims late one night, said we'd never make the grade, so he left to learn a trade".

It wasn't long before Ian and Laurence left too (neither had actually picked up an instrument), leaving just Martin and I. After that, we continued frantically writing more songs in my bedroom and in his Mum and Dad's front room. Sometimes a guest drummer would join in un-invited, in the form of the next door neighbour banging on the walls, he often adding backing vocals too –'KEEP THE BLOODY NOISE DOWN!!'

We wanted everyone to know we were a band, and so started writing the band logo everywhere, and then we had a brainwave to start our own fanzine up. We called it 'Stop, Look, Listen'; it was basically a way to create free publicity for the band with fake reviews and information about The Victims. We added some interviews and put a few reviews of other bands in there too. We photo-copied it all for a cost of fifty pence per issue, and then sold it for a bargain price of just ten pence a copy; we just considered it a worthwhile loss leader. We would take some copies to Barb's every week and sold around a hundred copies in total of issue one. Losing money, but gaining valuable self publicity.

Issue number two had to wait until 1980, but eventually was photocopied and this time we called it 'Support Your Local Punk Band'. Again we sold it at the gigs we attended, or swapped copies with other fanzine sellers. It was a great way of spreading the word about our band and building up a small following, sharing information and recommending great records, bands and gigs to anyone who would listen.

That summer of 1978 became a major rejection of rules and regulations because at last, exams were over, we were free, and school was out forever. I dug out my old Alice Cooper record and loved it to death!

In July my cousin Mike's band, City Boy, scored a major chart hit with the single '5705' which reached number 8 in the national charts, they appeared on Top of the Pops and followed it up with another single 'What a Night' in October, scoring another Top of the Pops appearance. They eventually went on to release seven albums for Phonogram and Atlantic Records constantly touring the U.S.A and Europe with a great stage show and a very loyal fan base. They had previously appeared playing live on Top Of the

Pops in 1976 with an earlier single called 'Hapkido Kid'; I thought it was all so exciting.

Well, school was at least out until September, putting on my recently acquired leather biker jacket I became a 'moped lad' on my Honda SS50 (which my mum and dad had agreed to buy me if I passed my exams), then roared off to Solihull College of Technology to start my A' levels. College was my parent's idea, as I had attained 5 O' Level passes. I was to study Maths, Economics, and Sociology. The maths lasted just 2 weeks as I found it way too hard at A' level, but sociology was great, more like a chance to chat up all the girls than a proper lesson, and Economics too was at least bearable. The highlight that made college fun though was the Common Room, it had a jukebox and a pinball table, this wasn't like school at all, and wow the girls, they were suddenly all grown up and curvy. I was going to enjoy this place.

Quite a few of my friends had recently got mopeds too, there was David White who we called 'Wally', (our short lived drummer), with his Suzuki AP50, Trevor Hughes and me with our Honda SS50's and, David Coombs with his Yamaha FS1E or ' yammy fizzies' as everyone used to call them. Trevor, just before he bought his bike, had actually owned an orange coloured Reliant Bond Bug car as he had found out that you could drive them on a provisional license; what he didn't realise was that the insurance companies wanted a small fortune to insure him, being so young and inexperienced, so he just used to sit inside it and pose on his dad's driveway. Oh how we laughed the day he put it in the garage and realised he was trapped inside, the top opened like a bubble car but the garage roof was too low to get out. To make matters worse it had no reverse gears either. Needless to say it wasn't long before he traded it in for a moped. We used to go on day trips to Stratford upon Avon and Earlswood Lakes or to nearby Lowsonford to enjoy a day's fishing on the canal, but the biggest fun we had was riding into Solihull and down to the end of Brueton Avenue where we had found out that Dave Hill from Slade lived. It was the last house on the right in the Cul-de-sac and poor old Dave hadn't realised he had bought a house right next door to a private girl's school, it was somewhat hidden by trees and a long drive way led up to it. Needless to say as soon as the schoolgirl's found out, he never got any peace. We used to love going up there and hanging around on the bikes outside hoping to catch a glimpse of him. I don't think we ever did though, but we did see his big iron gates with the initials D.H on them and his Rolls Royce in the driveway with his YOB 1 number plates. I guess we all thought that one day.....maybe just maybe.....It could be us.

On the television, and broadcast from the ATV Studio's in Birmingham that summer was a new music show called 'Revolver', so called because the stage the band's appeared on revolved, I had heard about the programme via my aunt and uncle as my cousin's band City Boy were lined up to perform, they were mysteriously mentioned by Les Ross, who in real life was a local Birmingham radio DJ from BRMB radio; he was playing the part of the burger seller/compére on the show. He announced City Boy as being on the following week's episode, but it must have been cancelled as they never did appear. However the program was full of happening local and national punk bands such as The Rezillos, X-ray Spex, Rich Kids, Buzzcocks, and The Stranglers, and local bands such as Brentford and the Nylons and reggae band Steel Pulse. The show was presented brilliantly in his sarcastic, witty, mocking style by none other than comedy legend Peter Cook.

Also there was another new show broadcast from Birmingham on BBC 1 at the time called 'Look Hear'. This ran from 1977-1981 and had a number of presenters including local Punkette and singer Toyah Wilcox. Two very interesting bands they showcased in 1980 were Neon Hearts from Wolverhampton and Misspent Youth from Birmingham, the later band had recently signed to local

67

label Big Bear Records and released a great single called 'Betcha Won't Dance', with the B-side 'Birmingham Boys' having been recorded live at Barbarella's.

Gradually it seemed the music scene was growing with the arrival of new sub genres. 'Punk' had been watered down by some bands into 'New Wave' or 'Powerpop', to gain valuable daytime radio exposure, the mod revival bands inspired by the dress style and sixties influences of The Jam were forming a revival scene of their own, and the new 'mixed' music of the Two Tone movement from nearby Coventry was breaking through into the mainstream charts in a big way. Not that this bothered us at all as we loved all the Ska music too, especially bands like The Beat from Birmingham and The Specials and The Selector from Coventry. But we are jumping ahead; first of all there was Christmas and the New Year to look forward to.

7/. GARRETT, 1979 AND ALL THAT

On January 9th 1979, Martin and I had been up to 'Barbarella's', to see if anyone was playing that evening and to try to get a gig arranged for The Victims, we thought we could maybe get to see whoever booked the bands in the offices above, but when we arrived, the door to the office stairs was locked, however we noticed the main club entrance door was slightly open with no-one seemingly around. We looked inside and saw lots of little one inch U.K.Subs button badges scattered over the floor, great we thought as we pocketed a few to later put on our jackets. Then we got brave and walked in, still with no one in sight, until two punks appeared and asked us who we were, they turned out to be Nicky Garrett, and Pete Davies from the U.K.Subs. We said "We are The Victims", have you heard of us? Obviously the answer was no, but they got us a drink and we started chatting. I asked if we could support them sometime, and Nicky said yes, and gave me a number for the tour promoter and said he would put our names on the guest list for the show that night, which was good of him, it was a brilliant night and amazing that the band is still going strong today after all these years. At the time of writing they are nearing their goal of releasing 26 albums, one for every letter of the alphabet.

When the man came to change the records on the jukebox at the college in June '79, I was ready for him!, never mind Meat Loaf and 'War of the Worlds', all I wanted was my red vinyl copy of 'Stranglehold' by U.K. Subs put on there, and nice guy that he was, he duly obliged. Every break, free period, and lunchtime, that record was played to death, in that common room, much to the disgust of the 'Normal's' as we used to call them; they were the studious types who used to talk about 'Lord of the Rings' all the time. We used to collect all our money together, get in there first and just play both sides over and over again. I must admit the novelty wore off after about a month, but there was no alternative, Abba just wouldn't do.

Martin was doing day release from the job he had found working at the 'Beatties' department store in Solihull town centre. My friend Laurence was also at college with me and so we enquired and found out that we could rehearse in one of the classrooms in the evening for free, therefore The Victims became a sort of virtual reality. Laurence rejoined and tried the drums, the best that anyone with no natural rhythm could, and over the course of a few weeks we had written about twelve songs that sounded vaguely musical.

We eventually got banned from rehearsing at the college as we were making too much noise and disrupting the night school classes nearby. It was funny though because we thought nothing of hauling all the equipment; Martin's Carlsbro combo amplifier, guitars and bits of drum kit onto the 92 bus, and by the time we had got it to college, we were knackered. One week, another college band called Gestalt played a show in the main hall, they were a rock band, but very good, we realised again we still had a long way to go in order to improve our sound.

Meanwhile the next day back at college, we were off on a day trip to London as part of the Economics course, to visit the Stock Exchange. Laurence and I wondered if we could somehow fit in a trip to the legendary record shop and label in Walthamstow, 'Small Wonder' Records. Sure enough we were given a couple of hour's free time during the day, and off we went in search of the shop on the tube. Little did we realise it was miles away right at the end of the line. It was well worth it though; we were like kids in a sweet shop, meeting Pete Stennett the owner and buying up all we could afford, marvelling over all the punk picture sleeve singles that just were not available in the midlands. He had just had a delivery of a new 7" by a band called The Pack, it was called 'Heathen'; it was the noisiest record I had ever heard, just brilliant screeching high vocals by Kirk Brandon and buzz saw guitar playing. Of course we bought a copy each. A quick look at our watches and a run to the underground station and we just about made it back into central London before the coach left for home.

Another time we went on a college study day-out to the West Midlands Safari Park at Bewdley in Worcestershire. After seeing all the animals from the safety of the college coach, we had some free time to visit the small amusement area. It was full of really tame fairground rides, but Laurence and I spotted a Ghost Train and thought it might be a laugh. It, needless to say was really bad, but had one of those netting type things that dangle over your face in the dark that is supposed to frighten you and make you think it is a spider's web. Being the lads we were, we went on a second time and decided it would be fun to pull it off. When we got to it, we both pulled really hard and managed to derail the car we were riding in; it came off the track and in a shower of sparks ground to a halt in front of a coffin with a glowing skeleton in it. We were both doubled up laughing, but sat there in the dark for what seemed like ages until the ride operative walked up to us full of apologies as to how such a thing could have happened! We both played innocent as we walked round the rest of the ride in the dark to the exit following him. Oh how we laughed later on the coach home!

After the ban at the college, we started rehearsing back at Martins house again, but we couldn't use drums because of the noise, and so Laurence soon lost interest and left again. Everyone used to talk about lining the walls with egg boxes as this was a cheap soundproofing method, but well, we didn't eat nearly enough eggs! The guitar and the microphone and sometimes the bass were all plugged into the same amplifier, but somehow we got by. We had heard that another local Solihull band, The Undertakers, had gotten friendly with the powers that be at the local 'Hatchford Brook Youth Centre'; it was a huge room, and they were often allowed to leave their equipment set up if it wasn't a club night. They had arranged it all to resemble a stage set too. Paul Hughes their guitarist was training to be an electrician and lent his talents to help the band build their own lighting rig, and of course fix any electrical problems with the amps. I remember they had a huge camouflage net as a backdrop that extended over the top of the back line of amps and speaker cabinet's, it all looked very professional to us. They had even purchased their own Public Address system to use at gigs, and had all this set up at the youth club too. All The Accused had at this stage was a Woolworth's 'Kay' guitar, and an 'Avon' bass, and a very over worked 'Carlsboro' Combo amp. We always had loads of attitude and enthusiasm though, and ultimately we just got on with trying to make the band sound listenable!

8/. HOLD THAT DIAL

At one gig by Angelic Upstarts and The Invaders at Barb's we bought a copy of a fanzine from Telford called 'Guttersnipe' and incredibly it had a review of our fanzine inside it. People were obviously starting to take notice, and so never ones to do things by halves, we decided to send our fanzine to John Peel at Radio One, and amazingly he mentioned it on air on February 6th 1979, saying that he had also received a letter from another band in Scotland called 'The Victims' that very same day, but luckily we had found out about the other band a few weeks before, and so had told John that we were now called The Accused, which he announced live on the air that evening. We hadn't recorded a note or played a gig or even had a proper line-up, but here we were being mentioned on Radio One to the whole country. The Accused were born. It is a strange feeling indeed to know that thousands of people were present at the birth, even if only with their ears. We felt that we now needed to move fast and get ourselves organised, being fully aware that John Peel would soon forget about us if we didn't get a tape to him quickly or at least send him a list of gigs we would be playing.

Four days before the Radio One mention for our fanzine, Sid Vicious died. He was both accused, and tragically became a victim as well. It somehow felt like punk was losing its number one icon, but in a strange way it spurred us on even more to keep the flame burning. Poor Sidney!

We needed a band with four members, we needed more equipment, we needed a record out, and we needed some gigs, oh and some money too!

I had a 7" single record at home called 'Where's Bill Grundy Now' by Television Personalities and on the back of the sleeve it listed prices and details of how to make your own record, and although there were words such as 'Mastering' we didn't understand, we were convinced we could follow their example.

It mentioned a record pressing plant in London called Lyntone Recordings Ltd, I contacted them and suddenly it all seemed to make a little more sense, the only problem was, we needed to raise three hundred and eighty pounds to make the records, as well as finding the money needed to record the songs in the first place. It doesn't sound a lot now, but that much money in 1979, when we were at college and broke was a King's ransom.

On Monday May 21st, the Angelic Upstarts played at Digbeth Civic Hall in Birmingham, and Martin Hope attended with some friends; when I next saw him he was covered in bruises, as some travelling skinheads had turned up from out of town and randomly started beating up punks, unfortunately for Martin he had inadvertently got caught up in the fracas. An incident of random violence, which had totally ruined what, should have been a great gig.

The next month in June, 'Wally', Trevor, Dave Coombs and I decided to go to Blackpool as Trevor had recently passed his driving test and bought a proper car, a Cortina. We were seventeen years old and it was our first real lad's weekend away, I can remember us drinking underage in the bierkeller on the promenade, knocking back the steins of beer and dancing on the wooden benches to 'Hot Stuff' by Donna Summer, funny what alcohol does to you!. When we finally stumbled out onto the sea front around 2am we had a hard job remembering which multi storey car park we had parked the car in. The original idea was to get a bed and breakfast house for the night, but of course by then we had spent all our money on beer. So when we finally found the car there was no choice but to spend an uncomfortable night sleeping in it, or at least that was the plan at first. We were all drunk and tired and then Trevor suddenly sobered up a bit and realised that another side affect of having spent all of our money was that we didn't have enough fuel to get home in the morning!!

In desperation someone came up with the bright idea of finding a local building site to look for some hose pipe to siphon petrol from another vehicle in the car park. Off we went again into the night and eventually miraculously found some rubber piping. With look outs posted, the sucking began (it was no easy job I can tell you, as the rubber hose we had found was really thick and not at all flexible) but somehow we managed it between us, each taking a turn. It took most of the night to do it though; job done, we all jumped into the car around 6am and made a hasty exit back to the M6 southbound. Oh the craziness of youth!

David Browne, was a lad I had met in the common room at the college, he told me one day he could play guitar, so I told him he could join the band, and that we were already radio stars, it seemed to impress him, so he was officially in, Martin switched to bass in theory, but in reality he hadn't got one, so carried on playing guitar as well, all we needed was a drummer, but such small matters didn't worry us , we were trying to get a record made as soon as possible in case John Peel forgot about us. As soon as we let it be known we were making our own record, I was getting people coming up to me saying things like "Oh my mates in a band" and "You should come and see my brother's girlfriends, cousins band play". Then it hit me that if were to make an E.P. like the Television Personalities, we could have four bands on it with a song each, and therefore split the production costs, brilliant idea!

It wasn't too hard to find the other bands for the E.P, first to come on board were 021, who I found out about because their manager Martin Frain was at the college too and he told me that they had been together for about a year and were gigging locally. Another name kept cropping up too; The Undertakers. They were local rivals of 021, but were recommended by Martin, he said they were a great live band and they sometimes shared a driver with 021 a guy called Woody. They had been around since 1977 (originally calling themselves 'Sid Syringe and the Undertakers') and known locally as a really tight and exciting live punk band. We then just had one more band to find and tried asking bands such as Dum Dum Boys (with a young Ranking Roger on drums), Life Support, Ha Ha Germs, A Mental Block, and Mass Media eventually settling on another band from the college called Cracked Actors, whose singer David Wright was a huge Bowie fan. Their bass player was Tony Mills who found some fame later on in the 1980's fronting the rock band 'Shy'. The story goes that I only gave the Cracked Actors about 3 days notice after the band 'A Mental Block' pulled out at the last minute. 'A Mental Block' later entered into the Melody Maker Rock and Folk contest on Sunday June 10th 1979 which was held at Barbarella's, the rumours were that they had won it, they were a much talked about local band for a while. I seem to remember their singer was called Richard Tibbenham.

Another local band that also were considered but somehow didn't quite make it were Mass Media featuring both Steve Ison who I had attended junior school with in Hall green, and 'Jock' (Alan Rodger) a well known drummer on the Solihull Punk scene who later played with Spizz, and also Martin Hughes who had joined Cult Figures and released the superb single 'Zip Nolan', on the Swell Maps' 'Rather Records' label in 1978.

The Undertakers, reputedly had recently been recording in Birmingham at 'Outlaw Studios' and therefore already had a song on tape they wanted to use called 'Illusions'. None of the other bands had been in a recording studio before, and with The Accused still without a drummer, I did a bit of research and found a small 4-track facility in Erdington, Birmingham, owned and engineered by a guy called Frank Skarth. The truth was that no-one had a clue about how recording studios worked, least of all me, but I figured to keep the costs down we would only need a few hours. My logic was as follows, 3 bands to record, average time per track, say 3 minutes, that's 9 minutes in total, add on a few practise runs, and some setting up time, I thought an hour per band should easily cover things, well I didn't know did I?

Previous to this I had wanted to record the E.P. at Horizon Studio's in Coventry as I had heard it was where The Specials recorded, and had actually booked the studio over the telephone for the three hours I figured we would need. I was dismayed to receive a letter from them a few days later which stated; "With regard to your recent enquiry and subsequent booking, I have spoken to our chief engineer and he feels, as I do, that three hours is insufficient time for you to record three bands playing one song each, we both feel that it is more likely to take in the region of eight hours to achieve a good enough standard to release on an E.P". We simply couldn't afford to pay for eight hours at the higher prices, therefore I cancelled Horizon and booked us into the far cheaper Skarth Studios.

Meanwhile David Browne came to a rehearsal and announced he had found us a drummer to play on the record. It was his friend Paul Perkins, who Dave assured me, was very good, and would be able to pick up the song very easily if we gave him a rough rehearsal tape. By this time we had actually decided to record 3 songs to put on the record, justifying the decision by the fact that they were all only a minute or so long, and well, the record was our idea.

On Sunday June 10th, 1979, all four bands at the same time descended on Frank Skarth Studios. It was like an army arriving, when he saw around 25 people on his doorstep, of what after all, turned out to be just a suburban house with a studio in the back room, his face said it all!

He then realised he had to record 3 bands in 3 hours and promptly told me it couldn't be done. However, around 5 hours later we were all finished and The Undertakers pre recorded track was added to the end of the tape. The studio was in Frank's back room and was only about 6ft by 15ft with a small control room. The band's filed in one by one, and recorded their songs while everyone else waited in the front room. I can remember everyone being bored, and at one point someone picked the phone lock, and started making phone calls at Frank's expense, I guess he didn't find out until the telephone bill arrived. When it was the turn of The Accused, we announced we wanted to record 3 tracks, and I remember Frank just laughed, but to his credit he just accepted it and somehow we achieved it in around an hour and a half. The results speak for themselves.

Martin and Dave both put down guitar parts, and then Martin borrowed a bass guitar from 021 and also laid down the bass lines. Paul Perkins the drummer never did get the promised tape to practise with beforehand, and therefore he had never even heard the band before he entered the studio. Basically he just put down a rhythm track for each song and somehow we just played the songs on top of it and hoped for the best. If you listen closely to the results he appears to be just doing his own thing, but somehow it sort of works, certainly a new approach to recording techniques. I don't think Paul was too keen on the songs though, as he was more into mod music and Tamla Motown. He had followed us to the studio on his Vespa scooter with a snare drum strapped onto the back, the route at one point taking us onto the motorway, which was totally illegal at the time as his scooter was classed as a moped. Our 3 tracks were put down namely, 'Solihull', 'Arrested', and 'Generation Gap', and mixed straight afterwards, it was only when we got home and listened to tapes that we realised that the start of 'Arrested' was missing having been clipped off during the mix, and that we had inadvertently missed out a whole verse from 'Solihull'. I had asked my school friend David Coombs to record the 'I thought Solihull was for snobs, but these punks think different' section at the beginning of the song 'Solihull', so David's part lasted 3 or 4 seconds and then he had to wait 5 hours for a lift home.

It had been a day of chaos, but this was what punk was all about, albeit unintentionally. Frank Skarth, the engineer, was amazed when we said 'Yeah, that'll do'. It sounds crazy now, but I don't think we actually listened to the overall sound of the band, being only concerned with our own individual performances. It turned out that Paul's drumming was quite interesting, but it definitely had little to do with what the rest of us were playing. The result was chaotic and brash and so all at once we agreed 'It's a take'.

The following day we sat down and listened to the other 3 bands, we felt slightly taken aback. They could actually play, although 021's manager when he heard their track rang me up and accused me of remixing their song '(Don't want to be a) Robot'; just for the record (no pun intended), we didn't touch it at all. I think maybe they felt the same as we did, that once it was on cassette and played at home it all sounded very different to how it had sounded on large studio speakers. At least the Cracked actors sounded musically competent, and The Undertakers with their 8 track studio tape sounded really professional. I found out what mastering meant and sent the tapes to Midland Sound Recordings in Balsall Common, Warwickshire to get the acetate cut. This was completed on the 12th June, then it was off to Lyntone Pressing plant in Upper Holloway, London where we first had 5 test pressings made, followed by a pressing of one thousand copies. When we arrived at the factory, one of their first questions to us was 'Where are the labels?' We hadn't even thought about labels at all, so we made a few phone calls and because of lack of money decided that blank white ones would have to do. These we ordered from Harrison & Sons in Hayes Middlesex and they were sent down to Lyntone by courier on June 28th. We collected the first batch from the pressing plant on July 11th, which were 14 boxes of 25 previously having been sent one box of five copies by post. Those five copies were test pressings that I don't think we bothered to listen to properly, we were just anxious to get some more copies back in time to sell at the gig we had arranged for the four bands to play, to promote it at Solihull Civic Hall. (See next chapter)

The day after the gig, my mum, on the morning of Tuesday 17th July came up to me and said with a somewhat horrified look on her face, 'There is a big man with a big juggernaut lorry outside the house, asking for you'. It was with great delight that a further 27 boxes of 25 and one box of 17 records were unloaded and brought into the house, and I rushed upstairs to play it, wow!, we had made a record, we actually had our own record! Listening to the finished product, I suddenly understood why record producers have jobs and why bands take months to make albums, but hey it was rough and ready and punk rock so who cared if the sound wasn't exactly hi-fi quality. I think that due to recording it quickly in a cheap 4-track studio and having so many tracks cut onto a seven inch single, the sound quality suffered a lot. We later learned that we should have, maybe, had it cut at 33rpm. Of course I played the E.P. to the family, and my sister to quote her reaction, uttered the immortal words 'What a load of shit!', but then this wasn't the Fleetwood Mac or Stevie Nicks type of thing she was in to at all. Although we knew the sound quality wasn't the best it could have been and we even wrote the legend 'Best in bad music' onto the blank labels, we were very proud. Each label was painstakingly handwritten in pen with many different variations. The one we sent to Radio One had 'John Peel Session?' hopefully written on, as did many others, and some said 'From the home of the Shirley Temple', this was a reference to the fact that John Peel had mentioned once; that on the way back from one of his road shows in Stratford Upon Avon he had noticed the strangely named Chinese restaurant in our home town of Shirley. Martin knew the restaurant owner's son from his junior school; he was named Cho Cho Lo. Martin would visit the flat above the restaurant to watch the television series 'Banana Splits' with him every week. Apparently they used to drum along to the theme tune using chopsticks!

9/. I SELL, WE SELL AND WE ALL START GIGGING

We were really proud of the record, all we had to do now was sell them, as a thousand records was a lot to have cluttering up a bedroom. It is also amazing how all your friend's then ring up asking 'if they can please have a free copy'. We were seventeen and now had some vinyl out, just like all the other bands John Peel played, wow! Each band received their two hundred and fifty copies, and I decided that The Accused label was going to be called 'No Rip Off Records', but advised the other band's to make up their own label names if they wanted too, this is why The Undertakers' copies had 'Black Rose Enterprises' written on, and Cracked Actors and 021 both created their own variations on the labels and sleeves too. We hadn't had professional sleeves made as the costs involved were actually more than the pressing of the vinyl records themselves.

I added a picture of 'Mell Square' (which is the main shopping precinct in Solihull), putting a spaceship above the post office, and some graffiti on the bench, and called it the 'Mell Square Musick E.P.' catalogue number N.R.O

Yaw 001.We never set an actual release date, but from July 17th 1979 onwards it was available. The sleeves were just made to order, (each time we sold a copy), purely because we were too lazy to glue up 250 copies in one go. I had contacted the local paper 'Solihull News', and told them all about it, and they published a piece titled 'Banding Together' with a photo of 021, mentioning the record and a concert, this appeared in the paper on June 30th 1979..

I had thought it would be a good idea to do a show with all four bands, to promote the record locally, and so contacted the large Solihull Civic Hall and duly hired the Charter hall out for the night of Monday July 16th 1979.It was only then that I realised this would involve P.A Systems, Mixing Desks, Lights, not to mention, Tickets, Bar Staff, a D.J, etc, I was quite simply very naive back then, but after all, this was to be The Accused' first public performance. It was all looking too good, I knew something would have to go wrong, and sure enough, unbelievably, Martin then told me he was on holiday that week in Newquay and couldn't do it. Paul Perkins the drummer on the record also didn't want to play as he didn't really like our songs. It was suddenly down to Dave and me, left alone with no band, a record just released, and a big gig fast approaching, to launch a rescue plan. Both of us in the usual Accused nonchalant way said "Oh, it will be alright on the night".

Enter Simon Baker, always known as 'Cockroach', (for reasons I have never found out), he was another friend of David Browne's and became our permanent drummer. Simon was so enthusiastic, but in truth had only recently started learning how to play the drums, taught to him by his younger brother Mark. Simon didn't think he could manage a full set on stage at such short notice, so it was agreed he would play half of our performance and then Mark would play the rest, a little unconventional maybe, but also a good gimmick for the band to have two drummers, even if they didn't both play at the same time. As for Martin, he went to Newquay on holiday, and we resigned ourselves to playing without a Bass player. We didn't care and really didn't think anyone else would either. With all four bands playing, you can imagine the fierce but friendly rivalry present on the night. The Accused were to go on first, as I figured more people would see us as they arrived, this was before I discovered the bar was in a different room. Then it was to be Cracked Actors, followed by The Undertakers, and finally 021 who argued that they should headline as they had sold the most advance tickets. We decided we had to do something special to leave an impression, because our music wasn't likely to, on its own.

We went shopping, visiting a local theatrical supplier's and purchasing some stage explosives. These were professional pyrotechnics that had to be wired up to a battery. We thought we had better test one out before the show, and so took one down to Shirley Park, placed it into a metal biscuit tin, attached the five foot long wire to the battery and BANG! The tin when it was finally located was about twenty feet up in an oak tree, the metal totally ripped apart. We quickly realised that these were pretty serious explosives, and so decided to place one on each side of the stage in the Civic hall.

On the night, right on cue, just as we started playing 'Solihull' they were detonated, the result being, we all went deaf, the ceiling turned black, thick smoke was choking us and the council later imposed a ban on the band from hiring out Council property in the future, I don't think they were too happy about the lyrics to 'Solihull' either, as it was, shall we say less than complimentary about the town. We hadn't yet written a full set of our own songs at this stage, therefore we had added cover versions of 'The Kids Are Alright' by The Who and 'Escalator Hater' by London based punk band Raped, 'Career Opportunities' by The Clash and 'Pretty Vacant' by The Sex Pistols, leaving just six original songs of our own. These were 'Solihull', 'Generation Gap', 'Arrested', 'Animal Experiments', 'W.M.P.T.E', and 'Police State'. We played 'Solihull' twice. Halfway through, on came Mark Baker and we changed drummers mid set as Simon only knew half of the songs. At the last minute we added a bass player too, I think he must have been a friend of Dave's, but to this day I don't know who he was and Dave's forgotten, so if your reading this and played that gig with The Accused, please get in touch (see photo section).

The evening was a big success, the only problem being that the bar was situated in a different room from the stage, which meant that half the audience were not present at any one time. I remember standing on stage swearing my head off, when I spotted my dad walking in, taking an interest in his son's talents, all I can say is he had gone by the end of the set, so I guess we certainly left an impression on him. There was a bit of trouble later in the evening when some members of the crowd took exception to 021 headlining over The Undertakers, but both bands eventually played great sets and The Accused had finally played their first gig.

Meanwhile in The Accused camp, Martin had returned from his holiday, and the band carried on rehearsing as a four piece. It was around this time that we discovered free publicity. On the way to Barb's, we had to pass through a subway that the local Birmingham bands had claimed, spraying their names on the walls. It sported such local legends as Suburban Studs, Killjoys, Spizz, The Sussed, The Clerks, Denizens, Dangerous Girls, and 021, to name just a few. Of course it wasn't long before the slogan 'The Accused Punk 79' appeared too. We printed up hundreds of small stickers with The Accused on as well and these were left on buses, lamp posts, and walls everywhere. People started talking about us and chatting to us in the clubs. I spent the summer running up a large telephone bill for my parents, ringing promoter John Giddings, to try to get The Accused onto the forthcoming U.K Subs tour starting in September, as the support act. Of course I used every trick in the book to get through to the man himself, and in the end he took my call and I confirmed to him that we had already met two of the Subs and they said it would be ok. Eventually he said 'Yes', that we could have the third on the bill slot at the show in Birmingham's Digbeth Civic Hall on October 23rd. We felt like we had hit the big time, as the U.K. Subs, since we had met them in January, had scored hit singles and appeared on BBC Television's Flagship music show, Top of the Pops.

Digbeth Civic Hall was a huge 2,000 capacity venue and the U.K. Subs had a big fan following, this was our one chance. We had to get it right for once. The talk was of hiring a big rehearsal space and some decent reliable equipment, and practising all hours of the day and night, but we soon came to our senses, we were broke!

However, we still had a big support show with a Top 40 chart band to work towards. It was still the summer holidays and we were enjoying life to the max, writing new songs, and attending lots of gigs. October seemed a long way off.

We went to see shows by each of the other three bands from the E.P, often playing at Solihull's only real live music pub, the Golden Lion. It was a great venue also known as 'Lord's Disco', and affectionately called 'The Lair' by the local bands that played there.

One memorable night it was the turn of the Cracked Actors, who put on an awesome display of theatricality and music, combining both elements to leave a big impression upon the casual gig goer. We hadn't seen anything like this before.....

10/. JUST THREE DAYS! – THE CRACKED ACTORS

I had met David Wright at the college and heard good things about his band, on the grapevine; I knew they had to be on the record, they had 3 days; David takes up the story:

The Cracked Actors by Singer David Wright:

"Richard and I got introduced to each other at college via a mutual contact Tony Mills, (who was to become our first bass player and later became a singer in the rock band 'Shy'), who was aware that we were both talking about forming a band. I was very much into Bowie and the Glam scene and Richard was very much into Iggy Pop and the Punk scene".

"We thought it would be interesting to form a group that combined elements of both genres musically, lyrically and visually, as this would create something different to everything else that was happening at the time. The band name came from the Bowie song and we *thought it had visual connotations to it, which suited our aims for the band".*

"We then recruited a lead guitarist (Adrian Barlow) and a keyboard player (Keith Rowe) and initially started to rehearse, through playing cover versions of Glam/Punk songs. At this stage we still didn't have a drummer!!!"

"Then, after just a few weeks, and really quite unexpectedly, Paul Panic approached us about taking part in the Mell Square Music EP, as one of the original line up of bands had pulled out at the last minute 'Okay Paul' I said, 'when do we go into the studio?'..........'Saturday' came his reply..........'Whaaaaat' (bearing in mind this was only 3 days away!)' you've got to be joking!'........... But, no, he wasn't".

"It was fair to say the midnight oil started to burn viciously as we decided that as it would be too risky to do a cover version because of copyright, and because we knew the other groups were all doing original songs, we had to come up with

94

one of our own to record, so 'Disco' was written and rehearsed within 72 hours".

"I suppose not many groups actually record and release on vinyl the very first song they write, so under the circumstances I thought we did a decent job. The lyrics were about a night out on the town (Solihull in our case!) and the disco scene that was going on at the time there".

"For the recording we had to borrow a drummer that Richard knew who learned the song on the way to the studio by tapping his drumsticks on the back of the driver's seat while I sang the song to him!!!"

"We then found out we had to record the song 'live' as a band, due to very limited studio time, onto 4 track tape which, again, was another shock". (I bet Pink Floyd didn't record Dark Side of the Moon like that!).

"Paul Panic then proceeded to promote the EP and one of the destinations for it was the John

Peel Radio Show, which went out between 10pm and midnight, Monday through Friday, on Radio one and was seen as 'the' happening radio show to get your record played on."

"They say everybody knows where they were when they heard Elvis had died (in my case a camping site in France!), well I remember where I was when I heard 'Disco' played on the John Peel Radio Show. It was a Thursday evening at about 11-30pm and I was washing up in an Italian restaurant (in order to bolster my Rock Star income whilst at college!!!) with the radio on, and I remember running into the restaurant and shouting "Hey, that's me singing on the radio!"

"Despite the startled looks of the diners they all stopped eating and listened intently along with the staff and the rather bemused owner for 3.19 seconds whilst 'Disco' wafted over the airwaves. Amazingly, I didn't get the sack and it certainly became a future conversation piece for those in attendance!"

"Paul then asked us if we wanted to help promote the EP by playing a concert at Solihull Civic Hall which we agreed to do, before starting to panic as we still didn't have a drummer. We asked the drummer who played on the record, but he couldn't do it as his Mum banned him from doing so. He was only 16 and she didn't want him to play in an 18+ venue!"

"Thankfully, it turned out that we were able to borrow another drummer, (Alan 'Jock' Rodger) from another local band (The Cult Figures), who weren't involved in the Mell Square Musick EP, for a few rehearsals and to play the gig for us as a one off".

"The set consisted of 'Disco' plus a few covers like 'I Wanna Be Your Dog', 'Hang Onto yourself' and 'Funtime' and we played for about 30 mins. Even though it was our first concert and we had only rehearsed for a few weeks we still put on a visual stage presentation, using props like a table to act as a platform to give the stage two levels for me to sing from, and elements of mime *including Richard and myself having a "fight" on stage whilst a strobe light flashed."*

"It was fair to say our performance made quite an impact on the 1,000 plus fans who attended the concert, even though it may not have been the most polished performance of the night."

"Things also got a bit tasty at the end of the evening as the running order of the bands had caused a problem. The Undertakers, who had been together quite a while (unlike the rest of us) and were the most musically accomplished, had the biggest following; they thought they should go on last. As they knew we had a trick or two up our sleeves to entertain the crowd they thought we should go on before them, after 021 and the Accused, to build the evening up as it went along".

"For some reason it ended up with The Accused going on first, us second, The Undertakers third, and 021 playing last, which left some of the audience suitably unimpressed and lead to some

98

of them invading the stage and a few fights breaking out!"

"After the concert Richard and I had time to reflect on where we were heading with the band and decided changes needed to be made. We needed musicians around us who shared the same vision of combining the energy and attitude of Punk with the imagery and theatrics of Glam, so radical changes were needed."

"We recruited a new guitarist (Pat Kelly), bass player (Andy Brennan) and, for the first time, a permanent drummer (Simon Benson), but decided to move forward without a keyboard player as we wanted to toughen up our sound."

"We also decided to write all our own songs, and only do cover versions as encores. Rehearsals began in earnest with the new line up and a few months later we were ready to start playing live again. We played at many of the well known music venues of the time, in and around the

Birmingham and Solihull areas, as we steadily built up a solid fan base."

David continues the Cracked Actors story..............

"One gig saw us headlining our own show at the Solihull Civic Hall where 500 plus fans turned up just to see us! (At this point we were still playing 'Disco' as part of the set, but we had musically re-worked it and renamed it 'Subway' with new lyrics with more of an American slant to them, now using Central Park in NY as the setting for the story as it unfolded)."

" During the following 12 months, whilst we continued gigging and building up our fan base, we released two further singles, The first was Statues / On The Line, followed by Rock 'n' Roll Fantasy / Calling For Time, both released independently by ourselves with limited pressings due to cost, and again recorded on 4-track tape live at the same studio as 'Disco'."

"After this period relationships within the band started to deteriorate (primarily due to personality clashes based on musical differences) so, even though Richard and I retained a good relationship, we decided to call a halt to the Cracked Actors and formed our own bands instead. Richard's was called Sport and mine was Pristine Scream. After about 12 months both of these had run their course for very much the same reasons!"

"Richard and I then realised we could be self sufficient. Richard was already an accomplished rhythm guitarist, but could now play lead and bass to a reasonable standard, and I had started playing rhythm guitar and keyboards for the purpose of song writing (from this point on all our songs would become joint compositions). Richard also bought a drum machine to help with recording ideas for songs."

"We realised we could move forward by ourselves and didn't need to put up with the negative aspects that other musicians can bring to the party when you try and create a

101

democratic environment for making
artistic decisions . So we decided to make a fresh
start under a new name (Theatron)"

"This meant two things. Firstly, we had to put playing live on hold, we said we wouldn't play live with backing tapes, we'd always want real musicians and, secondly, that our sound was to change as it started to move away from the Punk/New Wave vibe of our early recordings to a more Glam influenced kind of sound."

"Our song writing changed as well, the lyrics becoming more reflective and the music more complex, and this culminated in our next release on cassette tape in 1981. Both 'Caged' and the B side 'In Two Minds' ran at just under 6 minutes each, quite a bold move at the time, but as a result contain far more intensity and atmosphere, both lyrically and musically, and also reflected our state of mind following the problems we'd had with our previous bands."

"We then felt we were ready to play live again as Theatron, but this time around it was Richard and I calling the shots, with hired musicians, coming and going as and when we needed them. In the mid to late 80s we also performed under the names Theatre 21 and Panic Stations."

"During that period we experimented with a number of musical styles, most of which were unsatisfactory in their results, when we suddenly realised we had moved away from what we loved most, our Glam rock roots. So we decided to do something about it!"

"We again decided we wanted to be totally self sufficient. Therefore after having acquired a four track analogue home recording studio and a new name to operate under, 'Mighty Fly' (which we still use to this day), we decided to focus on writing and recording a complete glam rock influenced album in 'demo' format. This is exactly what we then proceeded to do."

"Due to cost, the plans to release it officially had to be shelved, so we then proceeded to write and record another album on a newly acquired 8 track digital home studio. This one we are hoping to officially release once we have applied the finishing touches to it, as financially it is more viable for us to now do that."

David Wright, Cracked Actors Singer

11/. KEEP HEADING SOUTH, RADIO STARS AND BUCKETS AND SPADES

So what happened next for The Accused and our big break?

Dave then decides to leave the band to live and work in Weymouth, Dorset. Money beckoned and he had got himself a job at the Gloucester Hotel on the sea front. We couldn't believe it at first, but what could we do?. Chaos once more reigned supreme in the world of The Accused. The month was August; we would have plenty of time to sort things out, well we were always optimistic. We carried on regardless; Martin, Simon and I, writing new songs and rehearsing the best we could, Martin swapped back onto guitar but once more we were bass less.

Towards the end of August, I had sent a copy of the 'Mell Square Musick E.P.' to John Peel at Radio One, but didn't really expect him to play 'Solihull' because of the swearing and the sound quality being so awful. Never the less I remember stopping in and listening to his show every night, tape recorder on standby, just in case he mentioned it. Then on the cold Wednesday evening of September 12th,at the beginning of the show after the familiar intro music, John announced that later on in the show he would be playing 'The somewhat muffled sounds of youthful Solihull'. Oh my god!, could it be us or was it to be Swell Maps again or possibly Life Support, another great Solihull band who had also recently released a single called 'Leader Deceiver', on their own 'Slug Records' label. My finger was glued to the tape recorder record button, and suddenly we were on, I was so excited I ran straight down the stairs, shouting to the family that I was on the radio. Of course I ended up missing most of it go out live, but luckily it was all safely recorded onto cassette tape. The telephone was ringing non-stop with each of the band's members calling me to tell me what I already knew, that we were now national radio stars.

John Peel played 'Solihull', swear words and all, and also 'Robot' by 021, and 'Illusions' by The Undertakers'. He said he would play the Cracked Actors the following week, and held true to his promise by playing it the following Thursday. The following is what he said on air:

"To quote from the 'Scene Around' column compiled by Lorna Bishop, (this was the Solihull News article we had sent in), If Mell Square suggests something as soothing as a trickling fountain, then think again!, it's the title of a new E.P. record by four young Solihull bands featuring New

Wave, Future Wave, and Disco sounds (a reference to The Cracked Actors track 'Disco', not the style of music).The four bands, The Accused, 021, Cracked Actors, and The Undertakers, have shared the £380 costs of producing the record, and are all set to promote it themselves by hiring out Solihull Civic Hall for a concert'. Still quoting John, he then goes on to say 'Well I think that's terrific and I'm going to play you three tracks from it, not featuring The Cracked Actors, no offence intended to them, I'll get round to their record next week sometime, but featuring the other three, starting with the Accused, and a hymn, an anthem if you like, to Solihull itself......"

John Peel then played the three songs and when they finish says "Well of course there will be those who will say, only 'Peely' could play that, and if that's the case then I'm jolly proud that it is the case too, those are three bands from Solihull, and I think it's magnificent that they got together and made their own record, I'm very impressed indeed, and there's a lot of people doing it, and I hope more people do it, the more the merrier, and Mike Read as you probably realise is starting to play some of these things as well, and well you know it's spreading, spreading...., the three bands there were The Accused, that was the first one, they did 'Solihull', and then 021, with 'Don't Want To Be a Robot', and then The Undertakers with 'Illusions', best in bad music it says on the sleeve amongst a great many other things, from the home of the Shirley Temple, and there's another message written on the record too, handwritten labels of course, says sounds bad to say the least, and of course the sound quality isn't perfect by any means, but that's not really the point, I think........And now Status Quo!!"

All I can say is "Thanks John Peel"; without you we would never have been on Radio One and that's a fact no one can dispute. Our memory of you and the fantastic work you did for new music, helping new bands, and the nations listening pleasure will be remembered forever.

After Dave had left we kept in touch by phone and he kept saying what a great place Weymouth was, and how the wages were great, and eventually he said he could get me a job too, for a couple of weeks in September, if I wanted one. So broke and bored I headed off down to the south coast by train to earn a bit of money. I was employed at the 'Gloucester Hotel' as a waiter, serving afternoon teas to the guests, also a porter and occasional bar man in the evenings. These times in my life I remember fondly, I was young free and by the sea, and getting paid for it too. Dave and I used to finish work, sit around in coffee bars, playing pool, and listening to music on the juke boxes. We often met up with Dave's many friends, most of whom were getting into the current Mod Revival scene that was happening in '79, with bands like The Chords, Purple Hearts, Secret Affair etc.

Dave became a Mod, and one day came back with a large red, white, and blue target tattooed on his arm. The talk was always about scooters, parties and records. I was never really into Mod Music, although some of the bands had obviously been influenced by punk as well, especially The Chords who everybody seemed to like. Underneath the hotel was a small venue that had touring bands on, unfortunately most of the gigs clashed with my shifts at work in the residents bar upstairs, but one band I do remember seeing was Martian Schoolgirls, who I later found included a guy called Dan Kelleher, who had previously played with Joe Strummer in the 101ers.

Our boss at the hotel was named Jethro and he told us one day he was a part time photographer for soft core glamour magazines such as Mayfair, Fiesta, and Penthouse. He asked us one day to help him move his stuff into another flat. As a reward he invited us to help ourselves to any magazines we wanted. He led us into a room with one wall stacked about four feet high and ten feet wide with glamour magazines. Of course we didn't need asking twice, we filled three refuse sacks, figuring we could sell them for a fortune, and transform the second hand book shops of Weymouth into soft porn emporiums.

We had an attic room at the very top of the hotel, accessed by the staff only service elevator, it was great we used to sneak down to the basement kitchens at night and 'borrow' bottles of wine and beer from the storerooms, dodging the chefs and kitchen porters. One evening we got very drunk, and with the magazines still unsold, ended up ripping them all up, and throwing them all over the place. We got totally drunk, drinking expensive wine, and eventually collapsed into a drunken slumber. The following morning, we were both ill and missed our early shifts, I will never forget the look on the maids face when she came in to find us, the whole room was carpeted with a sea of breasts and backsides.

I had failed to take my first year examinations at college, and much to my parents horror, had decided to drop out of education, to remain working at the hotel for a while, but during September, the U.K Subs 'Another Kind Of Blues' tour had started, I knew I had to return to Birmingham to rehearse for our gig with them at the end of October. Then I spotted in 'Sounds' that they would be playing in Plymouth on September 24th.

Dave and I decided to leave our jobs, and hitch hike along the coast to see them play in Plymouth at Monroe's club (previously known as Woods club). Dave had his electric guitar with him, and we had the idea of trying to meet up again with Nicky Garrett and hopefully talk ourselves onto the bill, just guitar and vocals. We arrived in the afternoon and hung around outside the club and finally spotted him, amazingly he remembered me from our previous meeting at Barbarella's. He invited us in to watch their sound check, but despite our pleading wouldn't let us play that night. He was however sympathetic to our cause and introduced us to their manager, who kindly said if we were willing to follow them to Exeter the next night, he would let us play a short set. We didn't need asking twice!

We boarded a train to Exeter and spent the morning frantically trying to learn a set of songs by sitting on a bench and busking to ourselves. It was quite a usual thing to hear acts such as Spizz Oil and Otway and Barrett just with guitar and vocals in those days, so we didn't have any worries at all. One thing that was slightly worrying though was Dave's choice of clothing. He elected to wear a Mod target T. Shirt and arrived in a Fishtail Parka coat too, but despite a few questions and odd looks no one seemed to care.

Exeter Routes club turned out to be much larger than the venue had been the previous night in Plymouth, and the other band on the bill was Lost Property, previously known as Fourth Reich, led by pocket rocket Punkette Nina Spencer, they would later became Manufactured Romance and release a solitary single. Nicky let Dave use his amplifiers and we opened the show to a packed crowd of punks, powering through the entire Accused set of songs, or as many as Dave could remember anyway. We got a really great reaction and came off to a lot of cheers.

We had planned on getting a train back to Birmingham after the show, but ended up missing it in all the excitement, and so headed for the station with some other people at around 1am in the morning. Someone broke into the locked waiting room of the deserted Exeter station to keep warm (they had electric fires in them in those days!), and within an hour the room was full of punks, all lying across the benches and the floor. We were soon spotted as having played at the gig; it wasn't hard as Dave had his guitar with him!!

I can remember being kept awake all night by drunken punks, who insisted on asking for autographs, despite our protests, and wanting to hear all about The Accused. One guy kept repeating that my lyrics were just like

'Shakespeare', I knew then he must be very drunk indeed, and realised I wouldn't be getting much sleep that night. It certainly seemed like a very long wait until morning and the first train back.

Dave and I came back to Birmingham, but it wasn't long before Dave returned south again to work in Weymouth once more. For me it was back to living with my parents and sister Susan, who was now in her last year at school, and starting to think about her exams. We now had under a month to get a line up together ready for the support at Digbeth Civic Hall with the U.K. Subs, there was to be another support band too, they were called Urge and came from Coventry; they had just released their debut single 'Revolving Boy' on the 'Consumer Disk' label.

Martin Hope was to be on guitar, yours truly on vocals, Simon Baker on drums (who had improved considerably over the summer months), and again a vacant position for a bass player with only weeks to go. Occasionally we would now rehearse in my bedroom, and being the resourceful band we were, Simon would use a padded kitchen stool and place 2 of the legs inside my dad's toolbox, this produced an improvised snare drum sound when hit with his hands, (try it, it's pretty good actually!). Martin had upgraded his Carlsboro amp to a 100 watt model, and was now using a

'Daion', Les Paul copy guitar. But what were we going to do without a bass player?

As the gig date came closer, large bill posters started appearing at all the main sites around the city with our name on them, and flyers too, in the record shops and even a large advert in the Birmingham Evening Mail. This in itself was funny, as now we were trying to find a way of removing one or two posters for our own bedroom walls, but that proved to be virtually impossible; the glue was too strong! We suddenly realised that the U.K. Subs were big news, they had been on Top of the Pops the previous week with 'Tomorrows Girls', and had also charted earlier in the year with 'Stranglehold'. We were to support a chart band at one of the city's top live venues in less than a month and we hadn't even got a full band, let alone one that had even rehearsed properly. Chaos was always the rule of thumb in the band though, and so once the initial panic had subsided, we resorted to borrowing a bassist from local band The Androids, his name was Nick Hartshorn. We had met Nick at a meeting of the Birmingham Music Co-operative, and he didn't need much persuading, when we told him who we were supporting, especially as now he could get in free. It was actually his first live show with a band. Later on, two other members of The Androids would become members of 021 notably John Croake and Mike Hancox.

The rehearsals went well and we quickly got a set of songs together, but we were trying to think up ways to win the crowd over. We decided to go for the unexpected and play a U.K. Subs song 'Telephone Numbers', in our set, this of course could be a suicidal move, either the audience would love it, or they would hate us for having the audacity to perform it. Our rationale was that either way it would be sure to cause a reaction.

The big day finally arrived, and our equipment was piled into the back of Simon's mothers Volkswagen Beetle, and we got the bus! Our gear was set up for us by the Sub's road crew. We then got to meet some members of the other support band Urge, who all seemed like nice people; they couldn't believe it when we told them that this was our first gig with this line up. We didn't get a chance to have a sound check, we were told to just turn up an hour before we played; I suppose they didn't want to have us hanging around the venue all day. On entering the hall and seeing the huge 2000 plus capacity crowd, I remember we all said, 'Oh shit'. The place was packed solid, including the upstairs balcony.

Our set was seventeen songs long which may sound a lot for a support band, but it only lasted about half an hour, I went and nervously asked Charlie Harper if he minded us doing one their songs in our set, he seemed amused and said 'Do whatever you want, it's ok with me'. It was time to enter the arena. We would either triumph as gladiators, or die like Christians thrown to the lions.

We ran out onto the stage, and instantly the spit started flying heavily and all of it in our direction. We started with 'Generation gap' announcing it was from our single, and I think some people actually laughed, the sound onstage was terrible; the audience were shouting out all sorts of things. About 3 songs into the set, I spotted Charlie Harper, the Sub's singer in the crowd, motioning for us to stop playing, I thought for a moment we were going to get thrown off the stage, but Charlie called back to the sound engineer on the mixing desk, telling him to turn it up and sort out the sound for us. As if by magic a few moments later the volume increased dramatically and became crystal clear, I could suddenly hear the whole band perfectly. I thanked Charlie from the stage and we launched into 'Solihull', the crowd were a bit more into it now. I was winding them up in between songs telling them about us being into chaos, and having no talent, we then played 'We're Crap', and watched as some lads ripped two plastic rubbish bins off the wall and threw them up on to the stage, one hitting the drum kit. We were certainly causing a reaction, but I got the impression most people didn't know what to make of us.

116

Still having to avoid showers of spit coming towards the stage from all directions, we pleaded for people to stop doing it, but we carried on playing. It was also just two weeks before bonfire night and someone on the side balcony threw a burning firework down onto the stage, luckily it exploded without incident, but hey this was getting scary now. I announced that if they would calm things down a bit, they would get presents, the sight of all those bemused faces staring back at me was priceless. Our thinking was that the Sex Pistols, had asked for presents from the audience in America, but we would do the opposite and give the audience some back. I told them that, hard though it was to imagine us telling the truth, we had in fact really got a record out and then I started throwing copies out into the crowd. All of a sudden it was a sea of hands and cheers, all trying to grab a copy. I think about 30 copies got thrown out into the crowd, but from that minute onwards they loved us, especially as we started playing the Sub's song 'Telephone Numbers', everyone singing along. This little ploy certainly did the trick and we felt we now had the crowd on our side powering through the rest of the songs and ending with a second version of our main track on the record 'Solihull'.

Exit one spit soaked band. I vowed to write a new song soon called 'Attacked by fireworks, saved by spit'.

Urge who were from Coventry, and of course the U.K.Subs, both went on to play great sets, but we were much too busy liberating the posters from the walls in the foyer to put up on our bedroom walls at home, success at last! The sight of four punks trying to hail a black cab taxi in amongst the departing crowd that night, in order to get Simon's brothers borrowed drum kit home was a strange sight to see! However, hey we had just played a gig in front of two thousand people, we felt like stars!

12/. LAGER, FORTY PENCE

'Solihull', our track from the Mell Square Musick E.P. (there were two other songs as well by us namely, 'Arrested' and 'Generation Gap'), was simply a big put down on the town, an anthem written to express how boring it was to be brought up in a place where nothing ever happened, "And no one cares for bloody us, in Solihull". It was a standing joke that for years the local council refused to even allow a fish and chip shop to be opened in the town centre, as they feared it would lower the tone of the area. The youth clubs all seemed to be closing down and there was nothing to do except hang around on street corners causing trouble. For the kids in the area too young to be allowed into the pubs and clubs, this was a daily occurrence. Even our local neighbourhood cinema had recently closed down in Shirley.

One week, not long after my family had moved into the area, I remember the cinema had a season of rock movies showing, but most of them were either X or AA certificates, I had persuaded my sister to come with me, but she was too young to be allowed in to see her idol David Essex in 'Stardust' or 'That'll Be the Day' so we went in to see the Pink Floyd movie 'Live at Pompeii' instead. I actually fell asleep; it was so boring; how I could have believed it would be anything else at the time, I really don't know!

The lyrics of our song 'Solihull' were actually adapted from a piece we saw in a college rag magazine from Burton on Trent Technical College in 1975, called 'This Bloody Burton'; Burton on Trent, the famous beer brewing town in Staffordshire was where my father was born and grew up before meeting my mother, who came from Tamworth. After they got married they relocated due to my dad's work to Birmingham. All of my Aunts and Uncles on my dad's side of the family and my grandparents still lived in Burton and I had been given the copy of the rag magazine by my Cousin, Stuart. I recently found out that the lyrics were originally written during the Second World War, and sung by soldiers about their very unpopular army posting to Halkirk in Scotland. This original version uses the 'F' word all the way through, but we had just used the word 'Bloody'; the original also contains many more verses than we used. At the time we thought we were adapting a student's work from the college in Burton. Our version though was as follows:

SOLIHULL

Solihull's a bloody cuss,
No bloody trains, or bloody bus,
And no one cares for bloody us,
In Solihull

All bloody clouds and bloody rain,
No bloody kerbs or bloody drains,
The council's got no bloody brains,
In Solihull

The bloody parks are bloody old,
The bloody seats are bloody cold,
The big posh houses, swiftly sold,
In Solihull

No bloody sport or bloody games,
No bloody fun, the bloody dames,
Won't even give their bloody names,
In Solihull

The bloody roads are bloody bad,
The bloody folks are bloody mad,
They'd make the cheerful bloody sad,
In Solihull

Every thing's so bloody dear,
It's 40p for bloody beer,
And is it good, no bloody fear,
In Solihull

Best bloody place, is bloody bed,
With bloody ice on bloody head,
You might as well be bloody dead,
In Solihull – I HATE IT!!

(Paul Panic – Trad. Arr)

It's November, and now we decided it was high time to go back into the recording studio to produce a new demo tape. We sort of had it in our heads that the next thing for us would be to release an album, we even had a title The Accused –'Standing Trial' .The idea this time was to record six new songs 'She'd Gone Punk', 'Bride just Died', 'Hellhole', 'London', 'W.M.P.T.E', and 'Photo-Copy Views'.

W.M.P.T.E. stood for West Midlands Passenger Transport Executive, which was the organisation that ran the local bus service. I booked Skarth Studio's again and this time it was to be Me, Martin, Simon and another borrowed bass player, this time Steve Clarke from Solihull band, Alternative Noize. The sessions went really well and we emerged with a tape of the six new songs ready to take on the world. Frank Skarth the engineer was ready for us this time and produced the songs in a much more professional way than the E.P, but still retaining that cheap punk sound from what was essentially a 4-track studio set up in his back room.

As Christmas 1979 drew closer, Martin and I became fully signed up members of a short lived organisation called the 'Birmingham Music Co-Operative'. To be honest the real reason we joined was because we thought it would bring the band more gigs, and because we were impressed that

123

Robert Lloyd from The Nightingales was also a member (The Nightingales had formed from the ashes of The Prefects, both bands being huge John Peel favourites). I think we only attended a handful of actual meetings, it always seemed like a great idea in theory, but in practise the meetings just seemed to end up with everyone arguing about venues, promoters, and everyone's lack of money. However in retrospect a lot was achieved in bringing many types of music to many local venues, and it served as a great way for bands to be in contact with each other and helped to keep a much needed unity within the Birmingham music scene at that time.

At the meeting on December 3rd, we met three members of a local band called Save the Sheep, and it was agreed they could support us at a 'Co-Op' gig to be arranged for February 3rd 1980. The venue was to be the 'Star Club'. It was to be part of a series of gigs arranged at the club showcasing local musicians from all styles of music; jazz, reggae, punk, mod, and everything in between.

I then got a phone call over the Christmas period, from a member of Save the Sheep, asking if The Accused would like to support them on January 25th 1980 at the Fighting Cocks Public House in Moseley. We of course said we would love to. We added a punk version of 'White

Christmas' into our set despite it being the end of January; well we thought it was funny! This was a really good start to the New Year. We had two gigs set up already. The only problem was that yet again we didn't have a bass player. Help was at hand again though, as Steve Clarke agreed to step in once more and play bass for us at the gig. The rehearsals went well in Martin's parents front room fuelled by non-stop cups of tea from his mother (Steve didn't actually didn't like tea, but was too shy to refuse; the contents of his cup ended up being poured into the plants!) We were to our own amazement, starting to sound really tight together as a band, and then the day of the gig arrived.

Disaster struck! Where was our drummer Simon? I made a call to his house on the way to the venue and he told me very apologetically that he was going on a scooter run and that he wouldn't be able to make the gig.

Simon had recently bought a Vespa scooter and Dave Browne was back from Weymouth, he now owned a Lambretta, and well I'm sure it sounded like more of a laugh than playing a support gig at a local pub, to go on a scooter run to the coast. Obviously the rest of us were not best pleased, especially as we had no notice, and we were now at the pub. Chaos reigned supreme again in the ranks of the band but 'it was Punk Rock; the show always goes on', we said it through gritted teeth.

The show became known affectionately as 'The Moseley Cock Up'; we went on to play, trying our best to make the most of a bad situation, minus one drummer! A tape exists of this gig, which although quite bad quality, is hysterical to listen to, we come across as just not 'giving a damn', but we did however cause a reaction as the loud applause mixed with cries of 'Get off', and 'You're Crap' on the tape testify. We always had a response to this though and simply started playing our song 'We're Crap', it always did the trick. The gig was somewhat marred by a very drunk member of the small audience who thought it was funny to keep approaching the stage and spitting at us, but he eventually must have got a dry mouth and retired to the bar, when he realised he was being ignored.

The Fighting Cocks, public house, situated in Moseley, Birmingham's so called 'Bohemian' quarter, has been the scene of iconic performances from many seminal bands over the years, from early punk bands such as Satan's Rats right through the spectrum to bands like The Smiths, UB40 and the Sisters of Mercy and local hero Ruby Turner.

It was a small room over the pub, but always lively with a regular crowd which in 1980 was made up from local punks, hippies, students and the ones we called 'The Straights'. It must have been because it was pouring with rain on the night we played, that very few people made the effort to attend, well that's my excuse and I'm sticking to it. I remember due to the lack of drums we started playing covers of Spizz Oil songs such as 'Platform 3' and '6000 Crazy', as they had never used drums on their early tracks either. Save the Sheep turned out to be a mod influenced band, but were rather good and very tight, totally the opposite to the chaos of The Accused. We looked forward to our next gig with them, they on the other hand probably started praying that we would split up before that happened. Simon had a lot to answer for that night, but being the sort of nice guys we were (and still are), we soon forgave him. When Simon returned however, with his many tales of the fun times the mod's had on the scooter runs, I think we all probably wished we had gone too, albeit it would have to have been on the coach. He told us about hundreds of scooters arriving covered in mirrors and how everyone had gone to some great club somewhere, pulling girls and dancing to great music. We learned the difference between Mod's and Scooter boys, Lamberetta's and Vespa's, Pro plus and Do-do's, ordinary faces and ace faces.

13/. MANY SUNDAY NIGHTS AT THE STAR CLUB

A lot has been written about a certain band playing at the Star Club, but of course, they were from Liverpool, and that club was in Hamburg, Germany. Well The Accused played the 'Star Club' too, the only minor difference being the venue of the same name in our case was a tiny little club in Birmingham. It too, quickly became a legendary venue for a few short years in the late seventies, and early eighties for Birmingham's real music lovers.

Situated above a communist, trade unionist book shop called Key Books, the club was in Essex Street, and it had been built in 1968 and used as an organisational base for many political campaigns, strikes, and demonstrations. Largely promoted by Frank Watters, the club was named after the 'Morning Star' Communist newspaper and had a diversity of uses, from allowing Arthur Scargill's Flying Pickets to sleep on the floors after the 'Battle of Saltley Gate' during the National Miner's Strike in 1972, to twice weekly Reggae Disco's during the seventies.

Sunday evenings in nineteen eighty however belonged to the Birmingham Music Co-operative bands. The venue was literally just the top room over the shop, about the size of an average family living room with a small bar at one end with a bust of Lenin sitting above it, and a small room behind to use as a dressing room. The steep stairs led straight up from the street outside. Everyone called it either 'The Star Club', or 'The Red Star Club', the correct name was actually 'Star Social Club', as evidenced by the sign over the bar. There was no stage; the bands would just set up in the corner, or in the middle of the floor.

Admission was usually fifty pence which you deposited in a plastic tub that somebody would be holding as you reached the top of the stairs. Once a band had attracted about fifty people the place looked full, and produced a great cosy atmosphere. Usually four bands played on the same bill, therefore it was virtually full before the public even arrived.

The Accused played there on three occasions, but we used to go and see other band's gigs there on Sundays most weeks. There is a wonderful piece of film footage that exists from around this time that shows John Peel visiting the Star Club to watch The Nightingales play, it shows the intimacy of the venue perfectly, and captures many well known faces on the Birmingham music scene at that time in the crowd.

Our first Star Club gig was the aforementioned support slot with Save the Sheep on Sunday February 3rd, which was a memorable gig with Simon Baker back on drums, but still no bass player (I think Steve must have been busy that night, or hiding after the Moseley experience!). I half jokingly asked if anyone in the audience wanted to play bass for the gig and was shocked when someone took me up on the offer and walked up onto the floor. We quickly borrowed a bass guitar for him from the other support band and he proceeded to play along with our songs as we went along. As most of the songs only had three chords and not too many changes in them, it wasn't too hard, but the brave crowd member deservedly got more cheers at the end than we did. He did very well, but I still don't know who he was, I seem to remember he just went back into the crowd afterwards, completely unfazed.

I would always wind the crowd up with comments such as "This song is for the A & R man in the corner from E.M.I Records, who has come all the way up from London to be here tonight to see us". The look on people's faces was amazing as they took in all my lies, some bought into the idea that The Accused were about to get signed to a major record label for a recording deal. Another good idea was telling the audience that "I am going to sit down because I'm bored", that one always provoked a reaction with many obscenities being shouted at us. If we weren't going down very well, we would start putting other bands down, or play bad cover versions of other people's songs. One such favourite at the time, guaranteed to turn a gig around, was our version of 'Do they owe us a living' by Crass, as it was full of swearing. It really did feel like playing a gig in your own living room at the Star Club, with the crowd variously seated on school type stackable chairs or sitting cross legged on the floor.

Again Save the Sheep performed a very tight, well rehearsed set of songs. If any of the old members are reading this, I still have your set on tape after thirty four years in my cupboard and very good it is too, so if you want to hear it, please contact me. The night was a big success and we were rebooked immediately to return on March 16th.

At this point on March 1st we had placed a small advert in the back of 'Sounds' music paper to sell some of the remaining copies of the EP that were still living under my bed at home. The big thing at the time was not to rip off the punks; therefore the advert offered the record for sale at the bargain price of fifty pence via mail order from my home address. By the following week I was in receipt of around fifty letters, the only problem was, I realised too late that I hadn't taken into account the postage costs of sending the records out, therefore we made no money at all, and more than likely made a small loss! However I sent a letter back with the orders advertising that we now had a cassette of new tracks available to buy, and that we were also looking for bands around the country to support us in their local towns. We were imagining playing up and down the country, how hard could it be?

Before the next gig, something monumental for the band occurred; one day I seem to remember, we were in Virgin Records in the city centre and bought the latest edition of a Coventry fanzine called 'Alternative Sounds'. It had been active on the scene for quite a while and in fact this new one was now the eleventh issue, I had previously purchased quite a few of the older ones and had found it to be a really informative read, usually with good and bad gig reviews from both Birmingham and Coventry venues and interviews with both big and small bands.

In fact Martin and I often travelled to Coventry, the W.M.P.T.E. used to have special bus rides there on Monday's for just ten pence. We had recently been to see The Clash play at Tiffany's on February 7th as part of their

'16 Tons' tour. We had also been to see them play the previous two nights at Birmingham's Top Rank Ballroom.

On the cover of 'Alternative Sounds' was the name of the other support band from the Digbeth show we played with the U.K. Subs, namely Urge, we were suitably impressed, and suddenly Martin emitted a shriek and pointed at a piece in the magazine, with a headline that said 'Accused Demo Single'. It was a glowing review of the 'Mell Square Musick E.P.'.As he read it out loud it soon became apparent that the reviewer must have caught one of the copies I had thrown out into the crowd at the Digbeth gig, and assumed all the tracks were by The Accused, easily done as there were no picture sleeves attached at that point, and also of course because they had white labels on which were completely blank, from a box of records we hadn't yet written on.

This was the review written in the fanzine:

"You were at the Urge/U.K. Subs gig at Digbeth, you might have been lucky enough to have one of these. If you didn't then perhaps it's in the shops. It's a six track E.P. and it is really good, the better side of punk rock. It has an absolute classic called 'Solihull' about the same place. It is worth paying pounds just for that one track. Although a lot of the time the music is raw and properly punk rocker stuff. They show their true depth of talent with a few strummy 'Mekons' type tunes, one about a disco. A Brilliant Record!

Written by Mark O

I love the bit about 'true depth of talent', little did the reviewer know that those songs were not The Accused at all, after all we were proud of having no talent at all. However to say that 'Solihull' was an absolute classic, and was worth paying pounds for, well what could we say, the man obviously had impeccable taste in music. We were buzzing with excitement all day, and started to think that a 'New Musical Express' front cover maybe wasn't out of the question after all; well we could dream! Then we woke up and started preparing for our next gig, back at the Star Club.

The next date was Sunday March 16th, and this time there was to be five bands playing, headlined I think by a band called T.V Eye who at the time had future Duran Duran member Andy Wickett in their line up, but it may also have been a band called Vision Collision. We were to play second from last, the other bands being '9.50', Degotees, and Media Macabre.

Simon's younger brother Mark who had shared the drum duties with him the previous year at the Solihull Civic Hall concert, now played drums for Media Macabre, and he introduced me to their singer the enigmatic Bryan Le Morte. They, as the name suggests had a penchant for horror imagery and had a great song in their repertoire called 'Grave Doubts' (I wanna be where the dead men are), a real sing-along audience pleaser.

The day of the gig came and this time the venue was packed to overflowing, as all five bands had brought friends and supporters, this time though we had an ace card up our sleeves, we had actually got a full band line up for once. A week or so before, Martin had asked his friend, Tim 'Ed' Eccles, who was a near neighbour of his, to join the band on guitar. Martin and Tim both called each other 'Ed', all very strange! The band rehearsed the best we could without annoying the neighbours around at Martin's house and found out pretty quickly that 'Ed' could actually play guitar really well. In fact he had even turned up to rehearsals one day with an idea for a new song. He played us the introduction and it sounded amazing, really intricate and musically challenging. It wasn't long before I had added lyrics and Martin had added chords, and we had a new song written. It was called 'What a way to go'.

We ended our set with this new song at the Star Club gig, and it seemed to go down really well with the crowd, it was almost as if they had heard the introduction to it before. Little did we know at the time that 'Ed' had stolen the complete first section of the song from 'The Cowboy Song' by Thin Lizzy. Of course he had neglected to inform us of that, and had claimed it as his own. The evening was another triumph and for the first time we had a proper functioning line up and actually sounded reasonably tight as a band. Once again afterwards, we were asked if we would like to organise another date to play at the club.

We arranged another show for the following Sunday, March 23rd, and we were told 021 were to be the headliners. We knew that they could usually be relied on to bring a lot of people along and we always could rely on our regulars too, we had a few friends who always attended our gigs. These were people such as our friends Steve and Nick from Alternative Noize, who always followed us around and who always shouted out encouragement from the crowd. There was Dave Coombs, who had recorded the 'I thought Solihull was for snobs' bit on the beginning of the track 'Solihull', and a young lad who always used to turn up from a local fanzine called 'Euthanasia'; his name was Lawrence, but known as 'Loz', he must have only been around fourteen but he always seemed to be present whenever we played. He was later to interview myself and Martin and the result duly appeared in his fanzines next issue. The funny thing was that in order to do the interview and produce the fanzine he came over and borrowed my mum's typewriter which was a really heavy iron one and he had to carry it home to the other side of Birmingham on the bus. When he did finally bring it back my mum was heard to say "I thought I had seen the back of that thing".

Another good night ensued, I think we even had the nerve to play our own tongue in cheek version of 021's song 'Robot', which we had cheekily re-titled 'I don't want to be in 021', much to their disgust or amusement. That cover came about because we always saw 021 as being totally organised, by their manager Martin Frain, we I suppose were more than a little jealous of this and therefore proclaimed that we The Accused, 'never did what we were told'. 021 went on to play a really well rehearsed set, and proved to us that they were developing into a tight exciting live band, now beginning to blend a few Mod influences into their sound. They also had been gigging a lot longer than us and this certainly showed. They seemed positively professional to our ears. Later on in the year in November 1979, Duran Duran played at the club supported by Vision Collision and The Detectives, and all for an admission of only sixty pence.

It was one thing getting gigs set up, but then we had to get people to actually turn up and convince them they should pay to see us. This meant that we had to advertise. At first we got some little white stickers printed with 'The Accused' stamped onto them and stuck them everywhere; on the lamp posts, all around school, and all over peoples clothes at Barbarella's. When we had a gig set up, we used to go to Saltley Print Workshop and get them to cheaply print us up a few posters on brightly coloured paper. It was actually quite exciting, as by putting them up in the city centre, we felt that everyone would see our band's name and remember it.

There were two major problems involved however: Number one, it's illegal to fly post, which when you have the band's name and the name and date of the show proudly displayed, kind of invites a visit from some official or other. Problem number two; how do you take a bucket of wall paper paste and fifty posters onto a number 92 bus without raising any suspicions? The answer to the last question of course is to persuade a friend with a car to let us hide the said bucket of paste in the foot well of the car, while they park on various double yellow lines, allowing various punks to jump out to perform commando style raids redecorating various city centre walls in the dead of night. Everyone was aware of the best poster sites, and therefore most posters were only visible for a few days before being covered up by new ones, especially if there was another gig on the same date at a different venue. It really was quite cut throat as to who was able to keep their posters up the longest. Our answer to all this was to be a little creative and find unusual spots to use, therefore the higher the better, up on bridges and road signs. Some of the really high ones stayed up for years to come.

021 at one point did actually get caught fly posting by the local council, resulting in a fine of around £20 (which was a big hit to the pocket, in those days), it even made the front cover of the Birmingham Evening Mail in 1982.

14/. NEXT DOOR CITIES

We were always very aware that it was potentially a career killer to only play gigs constantly around Birmingham and Solihull, and therefore we were always on the lookout for gigs further afield, to play in other cities.

Our friends, The Undertakers had recently set themselves up, a residency gig in Redditch and had forged some links with the emerging Two Tone scene happening in Coventry. They had even succeeded in getting Charley Anderson, the bass guitarist from The Selector to produce and play keyboards on one of their demo tapes.

Steve Clarke and Nick Knibbs asked us if we would like to support their band Alternative noize, who were now simply called Noize, at a gig they had set up at a Coventry venue called The White Swan. Naturally we jumped at the chance and so it was arranged for Monday 7th April 1980.

On the night of the gig we arrived to find that again, there was no stage, and so a large table had to be moved from an alcove area, to enable us to set up both band's sound equipment. Noize used synthesizers and bass, but didn't use guitar and were only a three piece; the sound they produced was really hard hitting and they had some very original sounding material, songs such as 'All the old Dudes' and 'They think we're on Drugs'. We had put a few posters up in Coventry city centre but when we arrived at the venue we found out that it was actually out in the countryside. To this day I have not been able to find this place again, I would presume it has been demolished, but strangely it doesn't even seem to exist on the internet, except for one small mention by Coventry band Criminal Class regarding a gig they played there in the eighties.

An audience of around fifty, which we considered not bad for a Monday evening, were present, and it was really good to play to new faces, in a strange town. All was going well until half way through our set, when the pub's fire alarm bells suddenly started going off. In what was another first for The Accused, we had to stop playing and go and stand outside in the car park with the audience. We had no problem identifying the cause because on exiting through the main doors, we saw a car on fire where it had been abandoned, presumably after having been taken for a joyride, before having been set alight in the pub car park.

Two fire engines arrived to put the blaze out, and we eventually played a couple more songs to an audience who

141

were now far more interested in what was happening outside the venue!

Around this time, we had started getting members of other bands approaching us at gigs asking us if they could support The Accused. We thought that if we put a compilation album of local bands together, that again, just like the E.P. we could split all the costs. A good twist to this idea would be to have one side of bands from Birmingham, and one side with bands from Coventry. I came up with the title of 'A Tale of Two Cities' (or was that Charles Dickens!) and started to ask bands that we encountered, to provide me with demo tapes of their songs for consideration. We received loads of tapes from some really excellent bands and tried our best to assemble some sort of a running order. The logistics of doing this, in theory is simple, but in practise you get all the bands ringing up all the time to find out what's going on. They all start arguing about who should be on the first track on each side, and then between themselves about which song to use. The project was to drag on and on for a while yet before coming to fruition.

I had become quite friendly with Bryan Le Morte from Media Macabre, although they had now changed the name of the band to Across the Room, and one day we both spotted an advert in the back of 'Sounds' music paper which read "Two young wenches seek musicians to form band, in Birmingham area". The 'wenches', bit did it for us and off we went down the road to the local telephone box armed with a supply of two pence pieces. The number we recognised as a local one and it was answered by one of the girls who we soon learned was named Shelley.

Shelley and Lorraine wanted to try and start up a band, although it turned out that they couldn't actually play any instruments, they were however, both trained dancers and used to work at a club in Sutton Coldfield called 'La Reserve'. We agreed to meet the girls at Bryan's one room bedsit in Stechford, a suburb of Birmingham.

Bryan as his name suggests; 'le Morte' being French for 'The Death', was very much into the dark side of life and indeed death. He had previously worked in Birmingham as a mortician and loved nothing more than to tell everyone all his morbid stories, and happenings from those years. When the girls arrived a few days later at his bedsit, he delighted in frightening them half to death, reciting spells, and telling them strange tales as well as showing them some animal skulls he had on his sideboard.

I wasn't present that day but Lorraine later told me that the atmosphere was very weird, with hardly any mention of music. Shelley wasn't impressed at all and her music career began and ended on the very same day. Lorraine on the other hand called me and asked why Bryan was being so strange, I didn't really know what to say as I didn't know him very well either.

Lorraine and I became great friends and started to think about resurrecting the 'Tale of Two Cities' project and making it a reality, but this was going to have to wait a few more months as The Accused were still my number one priority. Bryan and I remained friends for a while but eventually drifted apart and 'Bry' as he was now known went on to record a great demo tape of new material entitled 'Winter Songs' with Across the Room in January 1981. The session features a very young Miles Hunt later of The Wonderstuff playing drums on three tracks and Mario from The Undertakers on the remaining four. I am not sure that even Miles would have a copy of this tape, but it is good music, very haunting and full of atmospheric textures. It is unfortunate that Bryan's previous band Media Macabre hadn't recorded any of their songs, as again some of those songs were great, especially their anthem 'Grave Doubts' with his lyrics proclaiming 'I wanna be where the dead men are'.

15/. OUR NEW MODERNISTS

Our drummer Simon and ex-guitarist Dave, as previously mentioned, had both purchased scooters when the mod revival scene had started in 1979. Along with some like minded mates, they formed the S.S.C, the letters standing for, Solihull Scooter Club. Dave of course already had his target tattooed on his arm, and they wore the obligatory parka coats and smart suits. Some of the bands they were now listening to, had originally evolved from the punk scene such as The Jam and The Chords, who both had great energy and lyrics, but I found some of the other bands on the mod scene very wimpy sounding. One of the benefits of hanging around with the Mod's was that they always seemed to know of great house parties; sometimes we would meet up in the city centre at the Rendezvous Cafe in Broad Street, the details would be passed around in whispers and then we would follow the scooters (myself and my friend 'Wally', didn't have scooters, so we used to follow in his Ford Escort car), to house parties in the suburbs, where some unfortunate people had to contend with a small army of Mod's descending on their homes.

It was usually when someone's parents were away on holiday, and some of the damage that was done at those houses was unbelievable. At one, I remember someone actually trying to replicate the scene in 'Quadrophenia' where a scooter was driven across the front gardens of the houses, wheel spinning the grass into a muddy mess. It often resulted in neighbours calling the police to report the invasion of thirty or forty scooters in their street, and excessive loud music, late at night. The word would quickly spread, the house would empty in minutes and everyone would jump onto their scooters and ride off in all directions before the Police arrived.

When a bank holiday arrived, there would be a scooter run organised to the coast. I went to a couple of these, in Scarborough during 1980, I used to go dressed up in my punk clothes, and travelled up in the back of a Luton van; this was hired in case any of the scooters broke down. We would arrange to meet up with various other midlands scooter clubs on the way out of Birmingham, usually at petrol stations, and travel up in convoy, sometimes with around sixty or seventy bikes in a pack. I have to say the feeling of unity and exhilaration was brilliant. There was always a big rivalry between Vespa and Lambretta riders about which bike was the most reliable and who owned the one with the most mirrors or the slickest paint job. The local Police forces would be looking out for us as we passed through the different counties, and would often swoop for spot checks, looking at the road worthiness of the various machines. The unfortunate losers would then join us in the back of the van, alongside anyone who had already broken down.

I couldn't believe my own eyes the first time I arrived in Scarborough, the sight of literally hundreds and hundreds of scooters from all over the country, both parked up and circling around the town certainly proved to be an amazing sight to see. There were the Mod's with their Parka's, the scooter boys with skinhead haircuts and beer towels sewn onto bleached jeans, the sharpies with smart suits and ties, the rude boys, oh and one Punk! , that was me!

It was just like the scenes from the film 'Quadrophenia', a youth invasion taking over the town for the weekend, roaming the streets in packs and terrorising the locals and the holidaymakers. It wasn't long before I learned all about the specialist scooter types such as Arthur Francis 'S' Types and Skeletons. I proudly told whoever would listen that Jimmy Pursey from the punk band Sham 69 had been asked to write some music for the film at one stage, not that anyone cared, as everyone was far too busy getting drunk in the clubs, and listening to sweet soul music. Usually by the time the weekend was over and we were halfway home, the van was packed full of broken down bikes and sad looking individuals covered in oil. Those days were great though, a real sense of comradeship and not once did I get any adverse comments about being a punk amongst the scooter boys.

I was never into the Tamla Motown or Soul music scenes, but the new breed of Two Tone bands that had recently appeared in the charts from around the Coventry and Birmingham areas, playing politically aware Ska music, sounded really refreshing. I had been to see a band called 'Coventry Automatics' when they had supported Sham 69 at Birmingham's Mayfair Suite back in 1978 and they had blended Punk and Ska together in a totally new way, with their message of 'mixed music', it was bringing the diverse cultures of the region together to celebrate great new music sounds. Of course that band became The Specials who along with fellow Coventry band The Selector and Birmingham's The Beat and Madness from London had spearheaded the Ska revival and injected a much needed shot of adrenaline into the music scene at that time. The fashions changed with the times as well, and now the sight of pork pie hats, Ben Sherman shirts and Sta-Prest white trousers worn with braces and monkey boots was a common one, both at gigs, and on the streets of the city centre.

A youthful Mr Panic

My Sister Susan, Mum & I in Brixham, Devon

The Zits circa 1978

The Accused (Ed Eccles, Paul Panic, Martin Hopeless, Simon Baker) 1980

The Accused – 1st Line up – Solihull Civic Hall 1979 (Who is the mystery
bass player?)

151

Solihull Civic Hall – 1979 Dave Browne

(L-R) Martin Hopeless, Paul Panic & David Coombs at Lyntone Pressing Plant – May 1979

The Accused - Martin Hopeless, Paul Panic, Simon Baker & Nick Hartshorn – back stage at Digbeth Civic Hall supporting UK Subs Oct 23rd -1980

The two Punk Fanzines we produced in 1979

'Stop, Look Listen' (Left)

And

'Support Your Local Punk Band' (Right)

154

The Author – Paul Panic

On stage Digbeth Civic Hall Birmingham 1979

Paul Panic (Bottom Left) Dave Browne (centre) Scarborough 1980

156

021 (early days)

021 (later days)

157

The Undertakers (Hobs Moat Y.C. 1978)

The Undertakers 1978 ".... If they weren't a Punk Band then I'd say
they were out of tune . . ."

Lorraine

Legendary Undertakers / Eye Do It 'roadie' Dave 'Braman' Browne
(R.I.P.)

BUCKINGHAM PALACE

21st November, 1980.

Dear Mr. Florence,

Prince Andrew has asked me to thank you for sending him your record and has asked me to return it to you with thanks.

His Royal Highness is returning it because he is aware how much these things cost to produce and is sure that you would like to use this copy of the record for further promotions.

I hope you will understand when I say that Prince Andrew is unable to comment on the quality of the record; while I am sure that you yourself would never conceive of doing such a thing, the danger always exists of such opinions of members of the Royal Family being used for commercial purposes.

I hope that you will understand the reason for this disappointing reply.

Yours sincerely,

Adam Wise

Paul Florence, Esq.

Letter from the Palace 1980

160

Cracked Actors – Ultra Rare Private Pressing 'Statues' 7"

David Wright – Cracked Actors

Eye Do It - On Stage at the Fighting Cocks Birmingham 1983 featuring
David Browne (left), original Accused member on guitar.

Eye Do It (Rod Walker, Dean' Mario' Marshall, Sarah 'Red' Winsper,
Paul Hughes & Paul Panic.

The Accused/Bride Just Died 'reformed' (Rich, Martin, Paul, Chex)

Press Darlings-Cabin Studio's Coventry with Richard Wise far left

Press Darlings – Meet Terry Hooley

Press Darlings 1991 (Sandra O'Reilly, John Hassell, Paul Panic & Tank).

Heronimus Fin - Astoria London April 2001

Heronimus Fin - 2nd Album Cover 1998

165

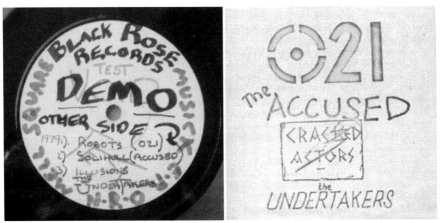

The 4 bands individually designed Mell Square Musick EP sleeves.

16/. PLEASE NO UNIFORMS!

Strange looking back, but in the early days of punk, there were certainly no 'punk' uniforms like there are today. A Mohican haircut was a very rare sight indeed. That style came to prominence with punk rock's second wave of bands such as The Exploited, G.B.H, and Discharge in the early '80s. Originally you would take great pride in making and adapting your own clothes, by spray painting slogans onto your shirts or ripping holes into them and safety pinning them back together again. Of course some people, who we would have called posers or weekend punks, would buy designer bondage trousers with bum flaps from trendy London boutiques such as 'Boy' or 'Seditionaries'. You could also buy similar fashions from a Birmingham store called 'Oasis market' which is still to this day, a labyrinth of small units spread over three floors. It used to have all the punk shops in the basement selling all the latest t-shirts, and if you searched a little harder, bootleg records as well, such as the Sex Pistols 'Welcome to the rodeo' and 'Gun Control'.

The other main Birmingham shop for punks was 'Kahn and Bell', situated in Hurst Street, and far more in tune with the real scene. This was run by Patti Bell and Jane Kahn; two fashion designers squeezed into a tiny shop, that later became the place to shop for the next generation of Blitz kids and New Romantics. The only thing we really wanted from there at the time was a fluffy Captain Sensible style jumper, but we could never have afforded their prices in those days. The shop was next door to a great record shop called 'Rockers Records' which stocked all the latest and more obscure punk releases and some great fanzines and badges too.

For The Accused, fashion wasn't important at all, we generally shopped in the Army and Navy stores or Birmingham Rag Market mixing and matching styles to try to look different. We sprayed up and made our own T-shirts, learning to use car paint spray cans, although for the U.K Subs gig I had actually used thick red gloss house paint to make a shirt which actually started to melt under the lights. All the punks in those days used to wear the little one inch button badges with their favourite bands on them, and pin them onto their leather jackets or army coats. It wasn't unusual at the time to see people with twenty or more badges attached to their clothes.

The other main record store we frequented on a regular basis was 'Inferno Records' in Lower Bull Street; they used to display all the picture sleeve seven inch singles, on the wall behind the counter which ran the length of the shop. We would go in and stand staring up at the wall for ages deciding which ones to buy. You could pick up leaflets from the counter detailing all the new releases and their best seller charts of the latest punk releases.

In 1981 they launched their own 'Inferno/Tempest Records' label and released singles by such bands as The Varukers and local heroes Drongoes For Europe and Dead Wretched. The shop was opposite a tiny pub called the 'Hole In The wall', and a few doors down was 'Woodroffe's' a large musical instrument shop. In those days record stores became the places to hang out with your friends to talk about the latest bands and records, those were the days when even the bigger stores like 'Virgin Records' in Bull Street had walls you could stick notices on, to advertise for new band members or to sell musical equipment.

Over the years Birmingham has had some great record shops such as Reddington's Rare Records, where you would spend hours searching for second hand bargains, or The Diskery, which is one of the 'last record shops standing', still surviving today in the city centre, it is virtually unchanged, since opening in 1952, although it has moved premises a couple of times over the years; where else could you shop for records and get offered a free cup of coffee while you browsed the racks. Others also worthy of mention over the years were Cyclops, Reckless, Virgin, Tower, Incredible, Second City Sounds, Rockers, Frank's Wild Records, Tempest, Vinyl Dreams, Icicle, Plastic Factory, Highway 61, Subway, and for reggae music Summit Records which was situated just along the balcony in the Bull Ring Shopping Centre from the wonderfully named 'Rollertoaster', a funfair themed fast food outlet that sold all the delights of the fairground, such as toffee apples, popcorn, candy floss and fresh doughnuts. The other two reggae specialist shops were Don Christies, and Baileys. Today we are left with very few Record shops at all, not even CD stores, it's all gone online which is a huge shame; we still have at the time of writing The Diskery, Swordfish Records, Music and video exchange and of course H.M.V. in Birmingham, but I wonder for how much longer will they survive?, even as I write H.M.V. has entered in and out of Administration and just escaped, to be either downsized as a chain or sold off, real music fans will watch with interest.

The other type of shops great for meeting fellow musicians, were of course, the musical instrument stores. The cheapest and best one in the city centre was Musical Exchanges on Broad Street; they used to have a logo on the door incorporating Dave Hill from Slade's, 'Super yob' guitar.

The second hand equipment in the store was piled so high, that just getting to the counter at the back of the store was like arriving through the two rock faces on the approach to 'Petra'. They also had an 'invite only' basement that was accessed by a tiny winding staircase which was like descending into hell, you had to negotiate a bargain and then a safe passage out again. Garry Chapman and Stu Clarke were the men to talk to in the shop, both at the time members of the rock band Cryer. The shop later burnt down in a fire and they relocated to much larger premises across town.

Just a few doors down from the original shop was the huge Bingley Hall Exhibition Centre, I can remember when I was very young my mum and dad taking my sister and I there to see the annual Ideal Home Exhibition or Boat Shows. We would happily run around collecting bags full of leaflets and free samples. In the late seventies and early eighties quite a few touring bands played there too, in what was really just a huge empty hall, somewhat similar to an aircraft hangar. I remember shows by The Runaways and The Jam especially; you can briefly glimpse me in Bingley Hall on their video of the 'Transglobal Express' Tour in December 1982, that is if you look hard enough! This too was destroyed in 1984 in a large fire. Other notable music

171

stores in the city at that time were Jones & Crossland, George Clay Music, Woodroffe's, and Chase Music.

Birmingham like any other large city had a large turnover of live music venues, with smaller ones opening and closing all the time. The main places to see live band's in those days were, in no particular order; Barbarella's (mostly punk), Rebecca's (punk), The Tin Can Club (alternative), Tresines (mod and pop), Golden Eagle (pub bands and new local bands), Barrel Organ (pub rock and later new romantic), Digbeth Civic Hall (bigger touring bands), Odeon New Street (large touring bands), Top Rank (middle range touring bands), Cedar Club (punk and alternative), The Outrigger (mod bands), West End Bar (teds and rock 'n' roll), Romulus (occasional gigs including an early show by Joy Division supporting Dexy's Midnight Runners in August 1979), and the Rum Runner (new Romantic). Smaller new bands like us though, generally played The Star Club or Peacocks in the wonderfully named 'Needless Alley'.

17/. QUEUE AT THE EXIT

Due to the success of the Star Club gigs, I received a call from the Birmingham Music Co-operative, offering us a chance to play at an all day festival of local bands to be held back at Digbeth Civic Hall on Saturday April 19th. We assumed it would be on the main stage, but after accepting, we found it was to be in a smaller room upstairs at the front of the venue. There were to be around fifteen bands of all musical styles playing throughout the day. I seem to remember we played around mid afternoon, again it was just a case of setting up in the corner, but at least there was to be an all day bar. There were jazz artists such as Jan Steele, and avant garde unorthodox bands like The Noseflutes, some reggae bands, The Androids, and us. I think basically we treated our performance as a rehearsal, as there was hardly anyone there at that time of the day. We simply bashed our way through our set of songs, watched The Androids, whose bass player Nick Hartshorn had kindly helped us out at the U.K. Subs gig we had played there the previous October, and left. However we didn't care because we had a big gig lined up for the following Wednesday!

Yes!, another famous punk band to support, this one had come about because rumours had started to spread amongst the local bands that Dexy's Midnight Runners, featuring ex Killjoys singer Kevin Rowland, had set up an office in the city centre for their management company, Midnite Music. Ever the optimists we tracked down the address to Needless Alley in the main shopping area and somehow talked our way into their office.

Dave Corke used to manage The Killjoys in partnership with John Tully, who was the manager of Barbarella's at the time, but Dave had now become Dexy's manager. He would later be released in favour of Bernie Rhodes from The Clash. We found Dave to be a decent guy who was willing to help us with our fifteen minutes of fame. He told us he was starting a new night at Romeo and Juliet's Nightclub in the city centre on Wednesday evenings to be called 'The Exit' Club. The idea was to put on touring bands and provide a D.J. to fill the club on a traditionally quiet mid week slot. He said we could play on the opening night April 23rd supporting the Cockney Rejects. The capacity was one and a half thousand people, we readily accepted.

Wow!, we had done it again, another major support slot, this time just the two bands, Cockney Rejects and The

Accused, and just like The U.K Subs; they too were currently in the charts with their song 'The Greatest Cockney Rip Off'. We were well up for it, of course, but we had heard that the Rejects had a large travelling following, who let's just say had a certain reputation for being very loyal to the band. We realised that we would have to be very good indeed on the night to get their attention and needed to be fully rehearsed and ready for any situation. The band was certainly much tighter and musical sounding now that 'Ed' was a permanent member on guitar, the sound was still loud and brash but now seemed to have a certain melodic quality amongst the bar chords.

Then Dave Corke told us that Kevin Rowlands and Helen from the management offices were going to attend the gig too. The pressure was now well and truly on for us because we knew if we pulled it off, it could lead to more important support slots in the future for the band. So on Wednesday April 23rd 1980, we arrived at the venue in the afternoon fully rehearsed and raring to go. The P.A crew had already arrived and had got all the gear assembled. It was a huge rig with full onstage mixing desk and monitors, and as the Cockney Rejects hadn't yet arrived, we were told we could have a full sound check. It was incredible, for the first time ever we could hear everything on stage perfectly, the sound was loud, powerful and crystal clear. This was going to be a great gig. I remember us all thinking that we had clearly moved up a level, heading towards the professional league.

We concluded the sound check and went out to get some food, and returned around five o'clock to be greeted with some very bad news. The Cockney Rejects had pulled out of the gig, as they had received a last minute call from Top of the Pops to record a performance of their single for the following days broadcast on the show. Already some fans were hanging around outside the venue and it soon became clear that a good number of them had arrived on the train from London especially to see the 'Rejects'. This meant we were in the unenviable position of facing an unhappy crowd of out of pocket 'rejected cockneys' with no main band to watch. We imagined getting bottled off stage, and possibly being blamed for the main bands non appearance. Telephone calls were hastily made to get a replacement headline act and we were told that Dangerous Girls, a local Birmingham band with a good following would step in and play. At the time we were gutted but at least the show was going to go ahead.

A notice was put up on the front doors explaining the situation and surprisingly most people decided to come in anyway, probably swayed somewhat by a generous cheap drinks promotion at the bar, and a rumour spreading around that the Cockney Rejects would be flying up to do the show after they had finished recording for Top of the Pops. The club was packed, the dressing room area even had showers, and a crate of beer was provided for us, so we relaxed a little and started looking forward to the show. Someone's girlfriend came back stage and told us that Kevin Rowlands and Helen had arrived and so we thought, right we will go on and give them all we have got.

When we walked out, the crowd were right up to the edge of the stage, shouting and chanting, and we received a big cheer. We launched straight into 'Generation Gap', and it sounded really loud and powerful. The stage was covered in what can best be described as Linoleum, which was really slippery and I soon regretted saying "You can 'gob' if you want to", a shower of saliva came flying from all directions, turning the floor into a balancing act between my legs and arms in order to simply remain upright. The whole band in their efforts to jump around as part of the show, were now literally sliding around. Simon's drum kit was on the move too, edging nearer and nearer the front of the stage with each one of his beats. We were, against all odds, going down really well, people seemed to be really getting into it and we were actually getting some people calling out for particular songs especially 'Solihull'.

Then while I was talking to the crowd in between numbers, apparently a young Punkette puked all down the leg of my army trousers.

I didn't actually notice this at the time it happened, and only became aware of it when we left the stage at the end of the set; everyone seemed to be keeping their distance from me!, I thought it was a bit strange until the rest of the band casually informed me that I had vomit all down my leg! I was very pleased then that we had showers in the room, and had the somewhat humiliating experience of having to hose myself down with the shower head. The gig though had been a triumph for us, we had proved we could play to a large crowd and win them over, we were elated, but those trousers of mine still smelt pretty bad!

Dangerous Girls went on and played well, but a lot of the crowd, I think, were expecting a band that was a bit more punk oriented. However despite a few unfriendly jeers, somehow they got away with it but didn't hang around long afterwards, fearing possibly more problems as they loaded up their big orange van surrounded by Cockney Skinheads. They kindly asked us if we wanted a lift home and we had to lie across all the equipment at the top of the van, but at least we were all still in one piece.

Two days before this gig on Sunday April 21st, Sham 69 had played at Birmingham's 'Top Rank Ballroom' and two local skinheads had become a bit boisterous on the dance floor, jumping onto each other's backs. This led to two bouncers wading in to ask them to leave. When the rest of the crowd saw what was happening they turned on the bouncers and a full scale riot broke out resulting in the police being called. The skinheads then turned on the police and were attacking them using broken furniture as missiles, a security guard was taken to hospital and the gig had to be abandoned. This resulted in three arrests and several injuries.

This however was nothing compared to what happened when the Cockney Rejects rescheduled their gig and played at Birmingham's Cedar Club on Constitution Hill about a month later. The Cedar Club was another of Eddie Fewtrell's clubs, along with Barbarella's and Rebecca's and this time they had brought their own support band with them from London. They were called 'Kidz Next Door' and had Jimmy Pursey from Sham 69's brother Robbie on vocals. A large contingent of Birmingham City football fans turned up and heckled both bands, taking exception to the bands promotion of their beloved West Ham terrace anthem single, 'I'm forever blowing bubbles', and the fact that they had previously worn West Ham football shirts on

Top of the Pops. Glasses and ashtrays were thrown at the band resulting in at least two members of the 'Rejects' being hurt and their equipment trashed, followed by an attack on the groups van. Mickey Geggus the band's guitarist was charged with GBH and affray as he retaliated, and the gig ended in carnage as members of the crowd were also hurt and running battles outside the venue with local youths also occurred.

Violent times indeed, we counted ourselves lucky to have escaped involvement in what could have been a potentially violent gig at 'The Exit'. Mod band The Chords played the club the week after us, and other bands lined up to play included Bad Manners, The Only Ones and The Members but as far as I can remember only The Chords played and then the club was no more.

Having met Dangerous Girls at the gig, we soon learned that Rob Peters their drummer had a small recording studio set up in the basement of the house he shared with the wonderfully named Fay Doubt, in Church Road, Moseley. We asked Rob to engineer a demo tape for us and entered the studio the following month in May, primarily to try out our new guitarist 'Ed' Eccles in a studio environment. We recorded a new version of our songs 'She'd gone punk' and 'Hellhole' this time joining them together in a medley style.

We soon found out that 'Ed' was indeed a really good guitarist. Hat's off to Simon too, who managed to perform a wolf whistle perfectly on cue on this track.

Meanwhile, Lorraine and I were still trying to assemble the bands for the 'Tale of Two Cities' album. Through our contact with 'Alternative Sounds' fanzine in Coventry we had put the word out for bands to send us demo tapes, and we soon had a large pile to start listening to. The same happened in Birmingham. We put the word out for bands interested and waited for the response. We would go to Coventry and meet people at the cafe in the Belgrade Theatre and get the latest news on who was hot and who was not. We soon worked out that this just wasn't going to happen overnight, as trying to organise so many bands and egos was an ominous task. Certain band's tapes really stood out from the rest and the likes of The Solicitors, Human Cabbages, Profile and especially Ideal Husbands were all superb bands from that time that had talent flowing out of their every chord. One way or another Lorraine and I knew we had to make the album happen.

18/. RIDE OF YOUR LIFE, IT'S THE BACK OF THE VAN TO WEYMOUTH

Immediately after the 'Exit Club' gig, we decided to raise the stakes and break out of Birmingham. We had been discussing the possibility of playing at seaside resorts around the coast of England since March, because we figured that in smaller coastal towns we would get bigger crowds, reasoning that there would be nowhere for the locals to go to see punk bands and that it would be like a holiday for us too.

With this in mind and following on from my experience of hiring Solihull Civic Hall, which I had found to be extremely easy, I had written to various places we had on our shortlist, places such as Poole Arts Centre, Brighton Pavilions, Bournemouth Winter Gardens and Weymouth Pavilion, hoping they might have smaller rooms in their centres that we could hire for a show. We became realistic very quickly when we saw how much they wanted to charge us, but decided to try it out in Weymouth as I knew the town from working there previously.

I thought that Dave Browne could use some of his contacts down there to distribute posters around town, sticking them up and spreading the word that the gig was on. The best reply I initially received was from Weston-super-Mare Town Council, who duly informed me that Cove Pavilion which I was trying to hire was in fact a model railway!

It was now May 17th 1980, and our local paper 'Solihull News' printed a photo and article about the Accused and the forthcoming 'two cities' album project. We were positively thriving on our 'Big' gigs and the publicity the band was receiving and then we got word that the Council had accepted our booking for Weymouth Pavilion. It was all set for Friday the Thirteenth of June, if only I had realised the significance of the date with its links to bad luck!

I decided The Accused would headline with support from 021, The Solicitors, Helpless Huw and local Dorset band The Skavengers, who were recommended to us by Dave Browne as being good local crowd pullers. We had tried to get Martian Schoolgirls at first but couldn't get a contact number to talk to them. The Solicitors, from Birmingham, I had met while looking for bands for the 'Tale of Two Cities' album and I had asked their singer Max Body to design the album sleeve, they were a highly original band who were starting to attract a strong local following in the midlands. They were later to change their name to Kabuki and issue a single called 'I am a Horse', before eventually morphing into Ausgang, signing a record deal and releasing a number of albums and well, check them out, their music is brutal; the rest is history. Helpless Huw was a local hero who had released a couple of singles on his own label, the latest being 'Sid Vicious was Innocent' which had been played on John Peel's Radio One show. His previous single 'Still love you (in my heart)', had been voted number twenty six in D.J. Kenny Everett's worst records of all time chart in 1978, high praise indeed!

I started to design another fanzine, our issue number two, to take down with us, but changed the title from 'Stop Look Listen' to 'Support Your Local Punk band', we had big ideas that it would spread the name of The Accused along the south coast once we had performed the perfect gig and succeeded in winning the crowd over! This time thirteen pages were prepared and ready to photo copy, but when I went up to the city centre the week before the gig to copy them, I found out to my horror that the public coin operated machine in the Bull Ring Shopping Centre was out of order. It sounds crazy now, but at the time I didn't know where else to get them copied, so it was abandoned and never made it to Weymouth. Oh how naive we were, looking back!

Strangely of all the places I had approached, Weymouth Pavilion was the cheapest to hire. Apparently they had a stage, a bar and a room with a capacity of eight hundred people, which we could hire for just eighty pounds. It seemed a good deal at the time and so with an admission charge set at just one pound, I envisaged a sell out, therefore making seven hundred and twenty pounds profit, easily enough to cover the travel costs and to pay the bands as well.

Something always seemed to go wrong at our gigs, but after the success of our recent shows, I couldn't fore-see any problems this time. All of the other bands were as excited as we were about finally playing outside of Birmingham.

It was strange that despite all the activity in preparing for this gig, the members of The Accused hadn't really been talking to each other a great deal over the previous few weeks, there wasn't any real reason for this; just that it was summertime and everyone was doing their own things. The week before the gig, disaster struck, with the news that The Skavengers had pulled out of the show; how dare they! The posters had already been printed up in day glo orange in nearby Dudley, and hopefully by now were pasted up on the walls and official council sites all over Weymouth.

After the initial shock I figured that at least the public wouldn't know and would hopefully turn up anyway. It then made me realise that actually, we were taking quite a risk playing so far away from home. After all we were four bands that most likely no one would have heard of before, doing a show in a large venue at the end of a jetty next to the ferry port, well away from the centre of the town. Well it was too late now, plans were far too advanced, the van had been booked and a small army of musicians were ready to invade the south coast. As The Skavengers had cancelled, I asked The Undertakers if they would like to play instead, and "Oh by the way, would their singer Rod mind driving the van too!"

Rod at the time was used to van driving and owned a red ex post office van which served as The Undertakers wheels. The funny thing was that outside of his house, there was a red pillar box on the corner, and often he would arrive home, park up the van, go to get out, and find some random member of the public thrusting letters or parcels at him, thinking he was the postman there to empty the box. Another time he had decided to start a window cleaning round with his cousin, but having attempted the first few houses, realised that being short in stature, he couldn't actually reach the upstairs windows to clean them, having, only at his disposal a small ladder.

The big day arrived, and what a glorious day it was too, beautiful sunshine, hot summer weather and a trip to the seaside awaiting us. Picture the scene, one white 'Luton' box van, four bands and assorted hangers on, most of which were pretending to be managers or roadies, equalling a grand total of twenty five people, (Helpless Huw and his band had wisely elected to make their own way down in their little Austin car), also five bands equipment, a rented P.A system, that took up half of the van space on its own, and enough bags and clothes to open a small shop. We were around an hour away from departure time and I was eagerly awaiting Rod's arrival with the van which had been hired from a local firm in Moseley, when the house phone started to ring. Thinking it was one of the band members asking to be picked up, I found myself talking to our drummer Simon's brother Mark. He casually informed me that Simon was sorry but he wasn't going to be able to make it today as there was another scooter run he was going on instead.

Hello, could I be dreaming?, yes it was a nightmare!, I was completely shocked; I couldn't believe that after all the planning, this was happening to us, the headline band, just an hour before we were due to leave. Being the second time this had happened on a gig day, I informed the others and we quickly realised it must be Simon's way of telling us he wanted to quit the band, but what a way to go.

In the great Accused chaotic tradition of the way things always were with us, we were determined to play on regardless, until I was then informed by Martin that 'Ed' didn't see any point in going now either. The band was falling apart all around us, and so what could we do, except go along for the ride, The Undertakers and 021 would have to fight it out between themselves or flip a coin to decide who would now headline.

Three people in the front of a van and twenty two more in the back, is not a good idea for a long journey, especially when a good three quarters of the available space in the rear of the van is loaded up with equipment. In fact it was also highly illegal as well, and extremely uncomfortable. Add to this the fact that 'Luton' vans have no windows in the back, just a metal roller door and a fibre glass roof which lets in a little light. It was impossible to see out.

Eventually after a short tour of Solihull, everyone had been picked up, and Martin and I became for a while, the butt of everyone's jokes, they thought it was hilarious that we had organised the whole thing, but now couldn't play. We had all taken provisions for the journey, cans of 'Skol lager' and 'Embassy' cigarettes, so no use crying over spilt milk, let's get drunk in the back, and enjoy the day out!

We arranged with Rod, who was driving, that should anyone need to stop for a toilet break, one of us would hammer on the top of the cab section as there wasn't any other way of communicating with the driver; this of course being years before the invention of the mobile phone. Rod agreed to this but warned everyone not to mess around while he was on the road. Without exaggeration it was only about an hour into the trip that it became unbearable in the back of that van; being such a hot day and with all those bodies in such a confined space, the temperature was rising by the minute, and it wasn't long before condensation started rolling down the inside walls of the van. Twenty two people drinking, breathing, breaking wind and smoking is not pleasant at all. Time sort of stood still as we couldn't see where we were or how far we had travelled at all, locked into our mobile prison cell.

After two toilet stops, brought on by the fact that everyone was drinking lager at ten o'clock in the morning, we had still only travelled around twenty miles, Rod was trying to remain calm and told us that he would not stop again until we had reached a motorway service station approximately fifty miles further on. Well of course the inevitable happened before too long; just as we had got onto the M5 motorway, Ian from 021, having consumed his four cans of 'Skol lager' already, said he couldn't hold on any longer. Choosing an empty bottle as the only receptacle available, he proceeded to relieve his bladder in full view of everyone in the van. The combination of drunken drummer and unstable surroundings could only have one result; an overflow. As the rivers of freshly passed urine meandered across the plywood floor of the van, seating arrangements quickly altered to accommodate for this new feature. Amps and cabs (manoeuvred to avoid the now torrent, as the beer can had fallen over) became small electrical islands of refuge as band members and followers alike fought for the best and most comfortable positions. The smell was disgusting, and the confined space and heat was making it worse by the second. Ian was pleading his case, saying there was no alternative as we couldn't stop because it sounded like we were on the motorway and hadn't yet reached the services. We all smoked in those days as well, and the confined space soon became smog due to lack of ventilation. Martin (021) Frain (always the manager) decided the best course of action was to wait until the smoke had cleared and then all light up together for the next cigarette. I'm not sure why, but at the time it had a certain logic. The combination of smoke, now stale urine, and hot sunshine warming up the inside of the aluminium sided van was a smell never to be forgotten, and even with young fresh lungs we all had some difficulty breathing.

Something had to be done and so it was suggested that we roll up the shutter a small way to let out the smell and smoke. We could also let in some fresh air, but we soon found out that the only air that rushed in was diesel fumes from passing trucks and cars. Still at least that was slightly more bearable than stale urine, despite the risk of carbon monoxide poisoning. Boys being boys of course, it didn't stop there and so the shutter got raised higher and higher, until all twenty two of us were staring out of the back directly at some innocent looking family in the car behind us, who were no doubt thinking the local zoo must be having a clear out. One car actually swerved slightly with the shock, perhaps the driver thought we were all going to leap out or something, meanwhile Rod in the front of the van was totally oblivious to the ongoing events at the rear, and I later found out that was because in the front they were all concentrating on a very intense game of 'Bogey

Roulette'. The origins of this little game reach far back into Undertakers history, the rules being very similar to the Russian version, but the loser in this particular match was Rod, who upon being wiped with the offending bogey, momentarily lost sight of the road in his rage. Snotty Punk rockers, indeed!

We rolled the shutter back down, fearing being stopped by the Police and toughed it out until finally arriving at the service station. What we didn't know until the van stopped and we lifted the shutter again, was that Rod had parked in front of the petrol pumps to fill up the vehicle with fuel. Mike Hogan was the first one out when we finally reached 'Michael Wood Services' and recalls watching what looked like a bank of fog drift from the back of the van as bodies emerged from the cloud of smoke, gulping for fresh air but actually inhaling petrol fumes. The poor garage owner must have thought he was seeing things, as just like a scene from some Hollywood zombie film, twenty two decomposing bodies came clambering out of the back of the van onto the garage forecourt with cigarettes nonchalantly alight and looking lost, mumbling about food and toilets.

Supplies replenished and bladders emptied, we climbed into our metal cell once more and gritted our teeth for the next leg of the journey. Cries of 'Are we nearly there yet?'

having turned into hollow wry smiles many miles back down the road. Dean and Mike from the Undertaker's were up on the top, over cab part of the van ripping up pieces of paper and dropping them down like snow onto Tony (021) Simpson's afro hair, this seemed to go on for miles before he realised his hair was full of white paper snowflakes. He was totally oblivious to their antics and to the rest of us; it looked like he had a very bad case of dandruff.

Weymouth should take around three and a half hours to drive to from Birmingham, therefore as we had finally set off around 11am and allowing for rest stops we aimed to arrive at the venue around half three or four o'clock in the afternoon. This we reasoned would give us time to unload the gear and set up the P.A. system and sound check the equipment before opening the venue doors to the public at around seven pm. What could possibly go wrong? Within another half an hour or so of travelling we found out. We felt the van turning off the motorway and slowing down and assumed we were turning onto some 'B' roads instead to continue the journey, but then we stopped completely, we heard the cab door slam, and the shutter being raised. A grim faced Rod was standing there telling us all to get out. Then we found out the reason we had stopped; we found ourselves at another service station, but this time there were clouds of steam coming out from beneath the bonnet of the van. The engine had overheated or the radiator had run dry, no one really knew, but of course everyone had a theory. We were musicians not mechanics, but either way there was certainly a lot of steam coming out of the engine as well as certain people's mouths.

One member of our travelling fellowship however, remained unconcerned and barely noticed the ensuing panic. All throughout this latest episode, while most people had gone for a cup of tea or a cigarette, there sat Viv Elmore from 021 wrapped up in his heavy sheepskin coat on one of the hottest days of the year. Perched on top of an amplifier in the back of that van unaware of the drama being played out in the real world, Viv was lost in the book he was reading 'The Hobbit' by J.R.R Tolkien. Viv had actually started reading the book as soon as we left Birmingham and had barely spoken a word since entering his safe haven of wizards and elves. We guessed he would put the book down in Weymouth play the show and start reading 'Lord of the Rings' on the return journey - 'There and back again!'

We were delayed on the services for around an hour but eventually, with the radiator fixed and miles of road ahead, the animals were rounded up and put back into the mobile zoo. The next hour passed pretty much without incident despite getting stuck in a long tail back of traffic for a while; up went the shutter, causing more astonished reactions from the cars behind us, as certain musicians reverted back to children and started the waving of various body parts at frightened motorists. At this point with the van going nowhere fast, Rod decided to try a few 'B' roads to bypass the traffic. It was on one such road that we came to a halt again; had we arrived in Weymouth? Not yet.

In fact we were in a quaint little village and we had stopped in front of a small sweet shop, the old fashioned type with jars of sweets lining the walls. Everyone piled out of the van except Viv, who was still no doubt residing in Rivendell, and Rod explained it was just a quick break. I felt a bit sorry for the old couple behind the counter in the little shop, suddenly being invaded by twenty odd people (pun intended!). At least their profits would most likely double for the day though, with the extra trade. It was only when we were back in the van that I discovered that certain members of 021 had helped themselves, and were now eating 'Mars Bars' liberated illegally from the counter display; Rod of course when he found out was extremely unhappy, concerned about S.W.A.T teams and helicopters that could show up at any moment.

Originally we were due to arrive in Weymouth at the Pavilion, at around four in the afternoon, but a glance at twenty watches as we arrived at the venue revealed the time to be nearly six o'clock. We had less than an hour to set everything up, sound check, and get ready for the venue opening at seven. That is the best thing about having so many people; plenty of spare hands to carry equipment into the hall, but trying to organise all of them in an orderly fashion however, is much more of a challenge. We had noticed that there was even a small line of punks queuing down the side of the venue, which was encouraging and meant that at least the advance publicity seemed to have worked. It wasn't too long before the gear was unpacked, assembled, and The Undertakers were doing their sound check.

My name was on the top of the posters being the promoter, stating 'Paul Panic Presents....' and it was in this capacity that I was soon tracked down by the manager of the venue asking me to ensure that the volume of the P.A system be turned down immediately, as it was far too loud. Strange I thought, I hadn't noticed? But I told him I would pass the information onto the bands.

I did inform their deaf ears straight away, but they were all too busy still arguing over who was going on when, and in what order, to listen and comply with the request. The posters were now meaningless. The Accused as original headliners were not playing and The Skavengers had pulled out. I was beginning to feel the start of a migraine coming on! The next thing to occur was that the manager came running over to me again, saying that if the music level wasn't reduced immediately, his bar staff had threatened to walk out. It soon became abundantly clear what had most likely really happened.

When I had originally booked the venue I had told them it was for the purpose of a public dance. They had even asked if we wanted a buffet table erected as part of the booking, so I guess it must have come as a shock when they found out it was five punk/new wave bands from the midlands. They thought it was just a regular function, but one look at the people outside and the way we all looked after three hundred miles in a van, and they had soon realised this was to be no ordinary dance. I was thinking; can these people not read? Surely the names of the bands on the posters should have given them a bit of a clue.

19/. SERIOUSLY, THE BAR STAFF ARE WALKING OUT!

"I did warn you!" the manager was shouting at me.

I was thinking how strange this was, had these people not heard loud music before? And to make matters worse everyone now seemed to be arguing. The bar staff really did walk out, but I think in the end the door staff took over the bar for a short while. The crowd were let in and Helpless Huw and his band took to the stage. Their set seemed to go down well and was very powerful sounding for a three piece band, although some people present compared them rather unfairly to The Jam. Next up were The Solicitors; the locals seemed to be enjoying themselves and the crowd was a mix of punks and skinheads, much happier now the bar was manned again. The Solicitors delivered a sort of early Adam and the Ants sound with lyrics full of sexual imagery and risqué subject matter. At this point Tony and Jimmy from 021 had started chatting up some local girls, hoping no doubt that they could maybe avoid having to pay for accommodation for the night, if you know what I mean! The only problem being, that the girls in question happened to be with the aforementioned skinheads who were now, not too happy about the unfolding drama.

The rest of us were standing around feeling really hungry, we hadn't eaten for hours having arrived late. "Wonder where the nearest chippie is?" someone asked, and so as soon as The Solicitors set was over, myself, Glyn 'Taffy' Rickards their drummer, and Paul, Mario, and Mike from The Undertakers, all left the venue to search out some local food outlets. We also intended to round up a few locals to let them know what they were missing, especially if we happened to pass any local punks or nice looking girls.

As soon as we left the building we noticed a funfair in the distance with a large illuminated Ferris wheel, and decided to go and investigate. 021 were to be the next band on stage at the gig, and no doubt due to the inter band rivalry between The Undertakers and them; it was deemed that the funfair was far more inviting for Paul and Mike. Of course by this time quite a few beers had been consumed, which made the experience of riding the waltzers and the big wheel far more exciting.

I can remember 'Taffy' and I at the top of the wheel saying, "This is fun, let's leave them all to it back at the venue".

The alcohol was clouding our vision somewhat as one ride after another was taken on with gusto, until we heard a familiar voice calling out to us and a figure running up to the fair, shouting that "we all needed to get back to the gig fast, as it was all kicking off!".

The figure was Rod Walker, the driver of our van, The Undertakers front man, who quickly became the voice of reason, trying to explain that during 021's set, beer glasses had been thrown and the skinheads were revolting. Apparently fighting had broken out and the management of the hall had called the Police. So with a few cries of "Oh Flip" or something similar, we all proceeded to run back across the town, to find on our arrival, a very irate venue manager and two Police officers, asking for a certain Mr Panic!

As I was the promoter and it was my name on the posters proudly proclaiming 'Paul Panic Presents....'I was duly summoned to the box office to present my case to the Police. Obviously as I hadn't actually been there during the trouble, there was little I could say in my defence. They told me they wanted to stop the show saying the noise levels were unacceptable, but I somehow pleaded the case for The Undertakers to play saying we had travelled a long way and that the local kids had paid good money to see the bands. I of course promised to get the volume reduced, which obviously in reality, didn't happen, and I was let off with a caution. I was soon to learn a few people had actually been ejected from the premises and were now hanging around outside the hall, laughing and joking and staring daggers at the security staff and the Police.

The Undertakers hurriedly took to the stage and played a great but somewhat shortened set of songs; the audience seemed to appreciate it and peace was soon restored. After their brief performance, the band eventually got talking to the local lads who had taken exception to 021's attempt to impress their girlfriends, and actually found them to be decent guys who were just getting into the whole punk thing in Weymouth. They told us how they appreciated our efforts and that they couldn't believe we had come down all the way from the midlands just to play in Weymouth. By the end of the night neither could we!

After having reloaded all the equipment back in the van and with me now suffering with a bad migraine, we realised it was nearing midnight and we had nowhere to stay, and even though a couple of the other band members had secured bed and breakfast accommodation earlier in the evening, it looked like the place of rest for The Accused and The Undertakers for the night, was to be the back of the van. O21 meanwhile had wandered off to take their chances in the town; Tony Simpson and Martin Frain had walked along the sea front, noticed a poster for the nights gig, proudly displayed on one of the councils official notice boards, and then spotted a covered sand sculpture on the beach. This looked like a free bit of shelter for the night, until the local police spotted them and they had to try and explain that they had just starred at the Weymouth Pavilion 'For One Night Only' frantically pointing at O21 on the poster. The police moved them on and eventually the pair found the rest of their band holed up in a dodgy bed and breakfast house, to which they then tried to sneak into without paying. Of course the landlady wasn't having any of this, and after a bit of an argument during which the first floor landing window got smashed, they were all turned out onto the streets to be faced with, thankfully, a fairly warm summer night on the sea front, or the rent free option of a nice cosy red telephone box to curl up in. Tiredness soon took over and it was time for some much needed sleep.

Max Body from The Solicitors remembers the day, in his own words as follows:

WEYMOUTH GIG

By Max Body

"Now, apologies in advance if the details on this are a little hazy – it was a *long* time ago – and either my memories of that day are sketchy or I've simply made some up. It doesn't really matter. What matters is, this was a gig that, *almost single-handedly*, made me quit the music industry altogether. *And I'd only just started! Well Almost...*"

"My first punk band was The Solicitors, formed by me and a bunch of school mates in Birmingham, (West Midlands, not Alabama, if only!). We knew f**k all. About *anything!* Not that it mattered. That was the point about punk rock: everyone was encouraged to do anything they wanted. So we did."

"Why on *earth* did the fine town of Weymouth decide to invite a bunch of Birmingham punk bands to play an all-dayer in their Town Hall!? Didn't they have any bands of their own? Did they owe Paul Panic a favour?"

"Paul organised the whole thing. I knew nothing of the details behind the show. It was enough to just turn up at a designated time and place, get in the back of a white Ford Luton van and drive south to Weymouth to play a gig. *Weymouth*, man! That was, like, near New York City or somethin', right?"

"Oh and yeah, you read correctly: *got in the back of a Ford Luton van*. Not just me, you understand – but something like 10 other bands. That meant about 1,500 individuals in the back of a Ford Luton van, along with drum kits and guitars, driving for around, 300 hours. For about 16 days. No windows, no ventilation, p*****g and s******g in the corner, because Paul had ordered", 'No stopping! If we stop, you will all just run off! I know it!'

"My girlfriend, Jo, was the only chick in the back. She was s*** scared. But I told her, its ok, baby, this is *rock'n'roll....."*

"Eventually, we arrived at Weymouth Pavilion. We thought it all very professional at the time – roadies busying themselves setting up the P.A. system for the sound check, Paul, liaising with the promoter and venue manager, checking that all was in order and that his bands were going to be looked after, and a substantial, lavish rider was going to be provided for his acts..."

"Of course, what was *really* happening was that some local kid had been pressured into lending another local kid his bass bins, a couple of microphones, bass and guitar rigs and Paul was asking around if anyone knew where the local chippie was..."

"I can't remember the playing order, but I *do* remember that we – The Solicitors – were The Best Band! God's F*****g Gift to Man! I didn't care two f***s about anyone or anything else. But that was punk rock, right? Also – Weymouth! You better appreciate the fact that we've come all this way to play for you!"

"Weymouth certainly showed their appreciation alright. By bottling us, I seem to remember not just bottles either. Bricks, Metal bars, soiled tampons and love letters."

"You..... (Expletives deleted)........... I roared, and leapt off the stage to knock someone's lights out. I clambered back on stage to finish the set. Thank you, Weymouth. It's been a real pleasure. Hope to see you again, soon!"

Got p****d,

Got back in the van,

Drove all the way back home,

Decided to quit being in a band,

Woke up the next afternoon,

Decided to do it all over again,

For the next 25 years. Only *then* did I quit.

King Hell!

The next morning Rod was up early, and eager to hit the road, but in those distant days before mobile phones it was time to launch a full scale search and rescue mission to find everyone else, to be followed by a nice greasy plate of sausage, eggs and bacon somewhere, anywhere cheap. It certainly had to be a budget breakfast, as the takings from the previous night's show would barely cover the van hire and petrol. And then we saw Martin Frain crawling out of a red phone box on the promenade, followed by Tony Simpson from another one, perhaps O21 weren't quite stars yet after all. With the rest of us crawling out of the back of a van, I guess none of us could have any kind of claim to fame just yet. However we all were willing to suffer for our art, or had we just heard that statement somewhere, and thought it was what was expected of us!

20/. THE JOURNEY NORTH

Breakfast over and suitably refuelled, both the van and ourselves, a pick up point was arranged and everyone was given half an hour or so to go off and get supplies for the long journey north, back to Birmingham.

Therefore with everyone back in the van, and with what promised to be another hot day, Rod put his foot down on the accelerator pedal and headed home, determined to get back in a quicker time than the journey south had taken. However it wasn't long before the natives got restless again, and using the tried and trusted method of banging on the roof to request a stop; residing in the back, remember, we had no other way of communication with the driver - a merry jape was plotted.

Mike Hogan and one of the members of 021, it turned out, had used their earlier half hour of supply time to visit a joke shop in Weymouth and procure certain items for their own amusement. It had all started off fairly innocently with itching powder being put down people's backs and then Mike came up with a master plan. He produced some fake blood capsules he had purchased, and said "Wouldn't it be funny if we staged a mock fight in the back of the van, and the rest of you could bang on the roof to make it look serious?" The idea, of course was intended to wind Rod up. For him to see blood all over their faces, when he opened the back of the van and have him believe that a fight had really occurred. Then the laughing could start, before letting on it was merely a prank.

Of course these things sound great in theory but what actually happened was that after banging on the sides and roof of the van for some time, Rod did eventually pull the van over, he marched around to the back, and rolled up the shutter; sussing out straightway he had been taken for a mug, and that it was all a joke. It quickly became apparent however, that we had stopped on a busy motorway hard shoulder, and he wasn't in any mood to laugh at all. He dragged Mike out of the back and a heated argument developed, resulting in Rod driving off and leaving poor Mr Hogan on the side of the motorway, much to the amusement of everyone else in the back of the van. After calming down, we had to travel quite a few miles to the next available junction before turning around to go back and pick him up. Needless to say there were no more unscheduled stops before we got back, but it didn't prevent a lot more itching and overflowing plastic bottles before finally a van full of punks rolled back into the midlands. Oh what fun we had, the day we went to Weymouth.......

21/. UNDERTAKERS

The Undertakers were always a great live band, with Rod Walker on lead vocals being a veritable dynamo, rushing to and fro across any stage he found himself upon. On guitar was Paul Hughes with his distinctive Shergold Masquerader guitar and powerhouse riffing. Bass duties and extra vocals were performed by Mike 'De Hoge' Hogan, and Drums expertly handled by certainly Solihull's best sticks man Dean 'Mario' Marshall.

The Undertakers often used to put on gigs at 'Hatchford Brook' for the local youth and soon developed a very loyal local following. One such follower and fan was a young girl called Jean Debney, who the band wrote an infamous song about. Her memories of those gigs and times as an ardent follower of the band after all these years are as follows:

My Memories – Obsession,

An air of surreal anticipation descended on the place, as the lights began to come up on the stage; the one or two carefully managed lumens that Cosmo could get his hands on. Then in the half darkness a figure emerged and presented himself to Moog synthesiser and began to produce the first notes of a Beethoven 5th at the same time in declaring in an almost demonic tone:

"Welcome to The Undertakers, a rave from the grave..."

At which point all hell would break loose, a cacophony of noise would overtake your senses and annihilate your eardrums. To the audience of assembled 13 to 15 years old, it was truly mind blowing; a cultural underclass of Bohemia which had arrived in Solihull, on the back of The Stranglers and The Sex Pistols as they had rocketed up the charts. We had our own punk entity in the form of the four who played on the stage, with their associated followers like the 'Potters' who broke the rules of decorum and were noticed. The 'boys'; Rod in his ridiculously tight leather trousers, which must have cut off all physical sensation never mind blood circulation and thought processes; 'The Hoge' a long time friend and leader of Alison's fan club (hence our association); Deno, an extremely talented drummer, with a quiet and withdrawn demeanour, self-assured yet edgy; and the 'love of my life' (at the time) 'Huges' (yes I have spelt that the way we pronounced it), a guitarist of extraordinary insight (unfortunately for me with the looks and arrogance to match).

For an hour, all in the Hatchford Brook Youth Club would go wild, as Rodney Potter pogo-ed to his heart's content, kicking anyone who got in his way. They would work through their set of covered punk songs such as 'Anarchy in The UK' to their own like 'Down to Hell', all were belted out at full volume. Rod Walker with his Fonz-like image which had adopted punk, Mike Hogan still learning to play the bass as he went along, Paul Hughes every inch the lead and Dean drumming to perfection almost anonymous and oblivious in the background.

And where do I fit in? I am not quite the infamous groupie, the Paula Yates to the Boomtown Rats that I have been painted, for I only went out with Rod for three weeks when I was 13 and shortly thereafter Paul for six, but having been mythologized I exist in my own right. And yes, I tattooed Paul's name on my arm with a compass during a particularly boring Maths lesson, and he broke my heart when he chucked me. My teenage adoration was my downfall, for I loved the band, I loved their attitude, their dress, their music, their sound. I loved their philosophy, for I was developing mine at that time, and the anti-establishment rhetoric was somehow more powerful, yet more futile, in such a middle-class affluent town. We could all be rebels because we had time to be, we could kick against the system, because we could afford the ten B and H and the bottle of 'Woodpecker', and walk round the streets discussing important stuff and singing 'Yesterday'.

For a while it seemed they could do no wrong, they were young and breaking ground at the right time, they outgrew the teenage groupies (like me) and headed for 'The Lair' and studio's and demo discs, they had a chance to make a mark especially when John Peel gave them some exposure, but then as these things often go, life overcame them, they grew up. As we all do when faced with responsibilities of paying bills and holding down relationships, sacrifices are inevitably made. In the same way they left their 'fans' behind down the Brook, the older ones were too fickle to stay, and you are only as good as your latest success.

But there was that song, the one that really could have been a blast and had all the possibilities to take them places. Written in a fit of 'piss taking' when I refused to leave a rehearsal. I had been around too long, my face didn't fit anymore, the new girlfriends had moved in. I was the uncomfortable extra, so I locked myself in the loo, and that was the moment it was born. Thirty four years later, I have to explain to my twenty-two year old why his mother's name is associated to such a song, makes quite a story, one I may write in a novel one day.

They were at their time, the best. They were a blast of rebellion in an uptight town, when we sat around Mell Square fountains, dressed in black, with shocking hair and dog collars, breaking all the rules, because that is what you had to do. Long live The Undertakers!

Jean Debney – "I am the resurrection"
xxx

The above piece was kindly written and given to me for this book by Jean, after I had managed to contact her again after all these years through social networking sites on the internet, she is now happily back in touch with the band! That song she refers to in her piece is the Undertakers song written about her entitled 'Who Killed Jean Debney', a local Punk classic.

The following is a personal history:

The Story of the Undertakers: by Mike Hogan

"The whole thing started at Hobs Moat youth club, Sheldon, Solihull. I was 13 at the time. Mario and I had a band called 'Impulse', he had previously been drumming in a short lived band called 'Shimmer', as did Rod and Paul, who were now calling themselves 'Syd Syringe and the Undertakers'. Mario and I had been in the 1st Solihull, Sheldon, Boy's Brigade, at the same time as 021's Tony Simpson had been in the 35th, Shirley section and The Accused' Martin Hope in

215

the 1st Shirley Scouts. The Club had a music room and it became apparent that we all shared a similar taste in music."

"The first rehearsal was held in Mario's mum and dad's garage and we all turned up with our gear. The P.A system consisted of a Slider Amp (so called because instead of knobs for volume treble etc, it had sliding controls) this kicked out a massive 15watts of raw power. You may laugh, but this was the most sophisticated piece of equipment we had, notwithstanding the gold Olympic drum kit owned by Mario."

"Paul had an old record player amplifier, driving a 12" speaker, it didn't sound too bad but the valves had a tendency to overheat and had to be fanned at the end of every song, Paul did this with an old union flag."

"I was playing though the extension amp and speaker to a Stereo system, and we both had very cheap guitars (no bass in those days). The first song we ever wrote was 'Down to Hell'. I'm not sure who wrote the chord sequence, but I know Rod wrote the lyrics, that's how the band started."

"We entered the Melody Maker National Rock/Folk contest in 1978 and turned up at the regional heats held at Warwick University with the other hopefuls. We did our bit as did the other bands, but what sticks in my mind is not the music, but the lack of food. Rod was the only one of us at work at the time, so the rest of us were skint. We hadn't anticipated how long it would take 20 or more bands to play and be judged, so we were totally unprepared for the day."

"Being slightly mischievous lads, Mario and I (followed by Rod and Paul) decided to have a wander, making our way upstairs and across landings, we finally arrived in what looked like a large meeting room with a balcony three storeys high, directly above the stage. After setting off the fire extinguishers and rearranging the furniture, hunger and fatigue set in."

"Looking over the balcony we could watch the other bands play, however this was not the main focus of attention, for on the side of the stage was a pie with one bite missing. We watched the pie for over an hour waiting for the owner to return to his snack, before heading back down stairs to eat the now stale cold pastry and congealed filling. Well it was the good old punk days, and ironically the winners of the 1978 contest were a band called The Losers"

"Rod was, and still is a fantastic front man. His infectious enthusiasm, energetic dancing and vocals, gave us the edge none of the other local bands had (in short no one else had Rod). Yes there were good front men out there, but none to match his natural appeal (especially with the ladies). The rest of us did the best we could to keep up with him, while learning our trade and developing our song writing skills."

"I remember one gig we did at a local youth club. The stage had been brought in especially for the event and was constructed from a series of boxes joined together and covered in a carpet. This would have been quite sufficient for most bands; however the constant running and jumping about the stage by Rod changed the structural dynamic somewhat."

"In one particularly energetic number the inevitable happened. At first I wondered what was going on, as the microphone stand in front of me suddenly shook and disappeared to my right and the carpet beneath my feet slid sideways sending me off balance. I turned and watched Rod sinking up to his waist between the boxes."

"Undeterred he continued to sing and dance as he clambered resplendent in tight jeans, kicker shoes and leopard skin top from the freshly made void."

"Most front men would have lost the plot, or at the very least been embarrassed, but Rod carried on like nothing had happened, even the band carried on without stopping. The crowd cheered and the gig was a great success."

"I didn't even know how to play the guitar, and tuned it to an open E and covered the neck with my thumb. After a year and a bit of messing about, the rest of the guys had had quite enough, and I was sacked for a couple of weeks before returning with a bass guitar and amp, this new dynamic kicked the band back into life."

"As I have mentioned Rod was the only one of us working fulltime, or bringing in any sort of a decent wage. Paul had by now started at the Rover Car factory in Solihull as an apprentice electrician, earning a pittance."

"I look back now with some regret that I didn't fully appreciate the unselfish commitment of time and money that Rod invested in the band. I was too young and full of ego to understand that the world owes you nothing, and too proud and naive to fully value what a great friend to us all he was."

"Every Saturday we would head into Birmingham on the bus to scour the music shops looking for equipment for the band, mostly at Rods expense, and mostly bought from Musical Exchanges on Broad Street."

"In those days, Musical Exchanges was a small damp shop, filled from floor to ceiling with second hand equipment. For years it had Dave Hill from Slade's custom built 'Super Yob' guitar hanging in the window. Even at the bargain basement prices offered, by far the majority of the stock was too expensive. Paul and Rod used to badger Garry Chapman (the part owner) constantly, week in week out, wheeling and dealing to try and get the best deal we could. Eventually a rapport developed and we were given access to the cellar. This was a dark dingy place serviced by a small narrow staircase, over flowing with antiquated gear piled deep and high, so that only the smallest of corridors was formed, illuminated by a single light bulb, yet to us it was Aladdin's cave. A place of dreams, imagining ourselves gigging with a proper PA system; we dragged out this and tested that, before (as tradition dictated) heading for the

Apollonia Cafe (where the Hilton hotel now stands) in Broad Street, Birmingham, to discuss what we should do, over a cup of cappuccino and a sandwich."

"It might seem that so far in this story I have painted Rod as an almost saintly character, but (as do we all) he had his bad points. We all had a firm belief in ourselves and the band, you needed this to do the job, however Rod took it to a whole new dimension."

"God help anyone who got his order wrong on the sandwich front. His favourite sandwich was bacon and tomato which he ordered every Saturday. I can still hear his voice though the decades to the owner of one particular cafe in Birmingham's Bull Ring Market area; when presented with bacon and raw sliced tomatoes, as opposed to the expected tinned variety, "Do you know who I am" he ranted "have you any Idea who your serving" A real Prima Donna."

"This became almost a trade mark with him, when any service level dropped below his expectations. We used to see it coming and would wind him up even more (Paul being the worst) until he went off into a tirade at the unfortunate recipient. Oh what fun!"

"We had no van at the time, so every stick of equipment purchased had to be shifted on the bus. The day we got the WEM PA system was a classic. Usually it would be a small purchase, a monitor, or an amp, which we could all take turns in carrying back to the midland red bus station, about a mile away from the shop. This P.A however was a different scenario. It consisted primarily of two 4x12" speaker cabs about 5ft high and weighing a ton each (they don't build them now, like they used to!)."

"If ever a band lived up to its name we did that day, as four of us carried what looked like two coffins across the city and onto the bus. Occasionally stopping for a rest and saying to passersby "he was a good un" and pretending to cry. Being broke also invoked a sense of resourcefulness and I recall walking to the bus stop in Solihull with Paul carrying his Vox AC30 between us, when we suddenly spotted a flashing light at some road works. As there were a couple we didn't think they would miss one, so picked it up and popped it into the back of the amp. The only trouble was that we didn't have the faintest clue of how to turn it off, and so we sat on the bus watching the back of Pauls amp flash on and off illuminating the luggage rack with an intermittent yellow glow, much to the amusement of the pensioners sharing the lower deck. It took two days to figure out how to turn the damn thing off!"

"About this time we had the pleasure of meeting one of the nicest guys you could wish to meet. Dave Coombes was the head youth worker at Hatchford Brook Youth Club. None of us actually used the club as we were all getting a bit too old for that sort of thing, yet we still had an affiliation due to the lack of funds preventing us from the frequenting the pub on any but the rarest of occasions."

"We had found out that the 'Smoking Beagles', a local rock band (a few years older than us) , used it for rehearsing at the weekend, and also when the club was not in use. After a few visits Dave agreed to let us rehearse on Saturday evenings in exchange for a few performances."

"I need to put this into context, our rehearsals were unsupervised, we used to collect the keys from one of Dave's colleagues and had free reign of the place. Girlfriends and mates used to come in to see us rehearse, you could smoke, drink, in fact if we hadn't been so serious about our music it would have been a party. Who could imagine that happening today, the trust given to us by Dave was seldom if ever misused, as we respected him totally for the faith he had placed in us."

"Dave's best quote was 'If I didn't know the undertakers were a punk band, I would swear they were out of tune'"

"Constant rehearsal started to pay off as our set list developed and started to grow. The introduction of cheap synthesizer technology enabled Rod to buy an Electro Harmonics keyboard. This was a small device about the same size as a laptop; it had a touch pad keyboard, was monophonic, and had sliding controls (these sliders seem to follow Rod around)."

Authors note: I'm sure Rod sold me the T.Rex album 'The Slider' once too!!

"The effect on the band was dramatic; it gave us another dimension with our sound, the type of material we could write, and also enabled greater opportunities to share out the vocal duties. By this time Paul and I were writing the lion's share of the songs. However it would be fair to say that the band as a whole worked together on the arrangements that gave us our unique sound."

"Rod still remained the front man but now had a larger arsenal to play with, playing guitar on some numbers, keyboards on others and most importantly engaging the crowd on all. I had little else to do but stand there and play and sound as good as I possibly could."

"Mario was like a whirling dervish behind the drums, not un-reminiscent of 'Animal' from the Muppets. And Paul, machine like, driving the whole thing with his distinctive guitar sound. To this day I haven't heard anyone play in the same style."

"Our popularity grew and we started to gather quite a fan following with regular gigs at 'Lords' in Solihull, based at the Golden Lion pub, and a residency at the Barrel Organ pub in Digbeth not to mention other gigs at venues all over the city."

"Of course we weren't the only band in Solihull, and were in competition with a number of bands within our genre. The main players were The Accused, a traditional Punk band driven by Paul Panic (our friend Flo), and The Cracked Actors, who had a Bowie influence. The Bass player Tony Mills had the voice of a drain pipe at the time and couldn't carry a tune in a bucket. It's amazing what a bit of practice will do. He went on to be the front man in the rock band 'Shy'. Signing twice for major record labels and touring the world. He's still a professional and now sings for a Norwegian Band 'TNT'."

"And of course our main rivals were 021, the Moriarty to our Sherlock."

"Tony Simpson was the front man and their manager, Martin Frain (also still on the scene in Glasgow, playing with Chomsky Allstars) was a force to be reckoned with."

"Despite our rivalry we all got on well. I wrote a song for them with Martin called 'Heaven and

Hell' and went into the studio to record it. I even ended up being their drummer for one night at the Star Club in Birmingham when Ian Richards was indisposed. Martin in turn contributed to an Undertakers song 'Too Blind Too See'."

"I may be biased but I think we pipped them to the post as the best local Band at the time. It's interesting though; last Year we had a reunion get together, the first in decades. We all sat around a table at Paul's house with Mr Panic to listen to the Mell Square Musick album, have a few beers and reminisce over old times. We listened to a few old tapes of live gigs and had a bit of a jam session. We got to discuss the other bands on the album, and guess what; we still seem to hold the rivalry in our hearts to this day. Paul Panic has it all on video."

"By this time we were all working and could afford slightly better equipment. Rod had bought a van, which enabled us to spread our wings and play all over the UK."

"We signed with a management agency on the Edgware Road in London called T&B Associates. They used to phone up Rod with various gigs and we would all pile in the van and head off down, or up the motorway depending on where we were playing."

"The Starlight Club in West Hampstead, London, comes to mind as an interesting gig. Rod, (always a victim to vanity) had taken a suitcase full of clothes to wear on stage. The rest of us just turned up with a change of shirt at best, but not Rod."

"The sound check went well as the P.A had been supplied by the headline band Fay Ray. It was nice to have a dressing room to change in as opposed to the gent's toilet and Rod took full advantage of the situation, trying on this and that and asking for our opinions."

"'Barking up the wrong tree' comes to mind; we didn't give a fig what Rod wore. We knew he would do his job so it didn't matter."

"The constant changing of garments and cat walk like antics went on for what seemed like hours; eventually we ran out of time and had to go on stage. Mario, Paul and I walked though the little door from the changing rooms at the rear onstage and picked up our guitars and drum sticks respectively. We started to play waiting for Rod to appear."

"Remember, Rod had a whole suitcase to pick from, including suits, jeans and an assortment of shirts too varied to mention, but no, none of the above was chosen."

"I saw Rod from the corner of my eye as he walked past me towards centre stage and he picked up his microphone just in the nick of time, (quite theatrical), but I couldn't quite believe what my eyes were telling me, as Rod commenced his act in nothing but a pair of transparent plastic sandals and a black towelling dressing gown that hung about 4 inches above the knee. I could hardly play as tears of laughter ran down my cheeks; Paul completely lost the plot and kept going out of time with the drum beat, and how Mario didn't fall off his drum stool in hysterics I will never know."

"It wasn't a massive audience, about 50 to 60 people stood in the small night club, but they certainly got value for money that night."

"A bunch of Canadians were in the crowd, both boys and girls, A number of the young ladies were fascinated with Rod's garb and after a few numbers, when we had settled down into our rhythm, curiosity got the better of one of them."

"Edging ever closer to front of the small stage, one girl finally plucked up the courage to find out what lay beneath and lifted the hem of the dressing gown. She turned and laughed. "What the hell is he wearing under there?""

"Please god, something!, don't let him be naked" screamed though my brain, as in one single move, Rod ripped off his gown exposing a pair of PVC trousers cut down to what can only be described as hot pants. Oh my poor aching cheeks. The crowd loved it and went mad."

"I had quite a high voice at the time and after the gig one of the Canadians came over to me and said 'Hey man I love your effeminate act'"

"Life's a funny thing, there was Rod gyrating around the stage in hot pants and it's me that gets called a puff. Not everyone thought that though, luckily for the rest of us."

"We never or very rarely booked digs (far too expensive), so we were usually dependent on the back of the van. It kept the rain off, but was always cold and it was extremely uncomfortable to sleep in, so being a bit of a talker, I was unofficially given the job of chatting someone up for lodgings."

"As I've mentioned, Fay Ray (great band) were the headline act and had the use of a flat in Kensington, a crate of lager and most importantly a female lead singer. It didn't take

233

much persuasion for them to invite us back. I was drunk as a skunk before we all got into the van to follow them and on arrival at the flat was led into a room with no tables or chairs, just people sat on cushions around the walls. In the centre of the small room was a crate of beer and a large number of ash trays spread out on a rug. The room was dimly lit, and a heavy smoke haze hung in the little air that there was, stinging my eyes. I'm pretty sure most of the people weren't smoking B&H, just inhaling the fumes sent my drunken head spinning."

"After about half a can of lager I had had enough and was led upstairs to an office with a sofa that was in the bay window. I was completely wrecked. Rod and Martin (his cousin) who was a roadie for us at the time were also in the room. I tried to get comfortable on the sofa, but the room then took on a life of its own, spinning and tilting up and down in my head. Without warning I could feel the vomit rising in my throat. The only course of action was to heave over the back of the couch. As I did so, I was hit on the back of the head."

"At first I thought I was being attacked, until I heard the uproar behind me, Rod and Martin were rolling around the floor in fits of laughter. The bay window behind the sofa had net curtains held into position with flower pots. In my haste to throw up my hair had brushed the curtain causing one of the pots to fall directly onto my head. Covered in soil, vegetation and vomit I promptly passed out to the sound of the still laughing cousins."

"I awoke the next morning to see Paul and Mario entering the room. 'You'll never guess what Hogan did last night' said Rod, 'why, what did I do?' I asked still not fully conscious, 'Look behind the settee' said Martin."

"So like the young fool I was, I did as instructed, and can still feel the embarrassment as a second pot was dislodged, striking me on the same spot and scattering its contents all over me and the floor."

"Obviously there are many stories covering the years we were together, but as the saying tells us, 'all good things must come to an end'. Eventually after a lack lustre period we played our last gig at the 'Yew tree' pub in Yardley, Birmingham in 1982. There were many reasons behind the split but in the end I just decided to call it a day. I had grown up with the band and felt the time was right to spread my wings and see how I would do on my own."

"We all went on to play with other bands or undertook solo projects with varying degrees of success, and most of us still play today. I now run a choir for drunken reprobates that sing at charity events and old people's homes."

"But I can look back at those days with great affection. The best days of my life! –"

Mike 'De Hoge' Hogan (The Undertakers - Bass Player)

In the early days of the band, The Undertakers had briefly been a five piece, with the addition of a lead guitarist, called Roger Springer. Here are some memories from Roger:

"I have some very fond memories of playing with the guys in the Undertakers in the mid-late 70's; In fact it was the first band I played in, in which I also played my first gig."

"I used to be in a class with Mario's sister at school, I knew her brother was playing in a band and I would constantly pester her, asking if her brother's band needed a lead guitarist."

"I don't think they were actually looking for another guitarist at the time, but because I asked that many times, I think they felt obliged to give me an audition.
I went along one Sunday afternoon to audition with them, I had not even heard the guys play, but they were well known and had a following, I didn't know any of the songs, but just improvised solo's as and when Rod gave me the nod to do

so, they must have liked what I did as they asked me to join them.

The next day (Monday), I met with the band at Rod's house and learned the Set over the next couple of Days."

"We also played a local heat of 'Battle of the Bands' at Warwick University.

There were about 40 bands on. I remember the sound guy did not have a clue what he was doing, every band had a terrible mix, when we came on we did 3 songs, by the time we got to the last song we had had enough, we couldn't hear anything, in the end we completely screwed the last song up and just stopped playing, Paul went up to the Mic and said "that's all folks", we walked off laughing. Rod told the sound engineer he couldn't mix a cake let alone a band."

"We regularly played at Hatchford Brook Youth Club, and possibly Hobs Moat Youth Club, definitely the Golden Lion in Solihull, and I am sure we played Solihull Civic Hall."

"I only played with the Undertakers for about 6 months I think; even though I loved all the guys I wanted to do more 'melodic rock'"

"I was asked to audition for a band named 'Rah' and felt more comfortable going down this route (audiences at melodic rock gigs didn't spit at you).I have not seen the guys for maybe over 25yrs, I hope they are all still playing and doing what they do best, although I bet Rod can't run around like he used too!
Dean (Mario), I was closest too I think, smashing guy, and a solid drummer.
Mike, I always remember had a great ear for melody, he could hear something and instantly harmonize to it, and Paul was a great rhythm guitarist, I remember his Vox AC30 being twice as loud as my Marshall 100w head."
Fond memories indeed!

Roger Springer- Early guitarist - The Undertakers

The Undertakers, 021, and the Cracked Actors continued gigging throughout the rest of 1980, and into 1981, playing both in and around Birmingham and Solihull; The Undertakers eventually catching the eye of a London based management/booking Agency, which resulted in a few shows in the capital notably the 'Moonlight Club' and such far flung places as Great Yarmouth's 'Big Apple' club and Redditch 'Winyates' pub. They played with many local bands such as Model Mania and Helpless Huw. A tour for the band was set up to be called the 'Dead on Arrival' tour but for one reason or another only a handful of the intended dates came to pass.

22/. VIVA 021

021 too, had become an accomplished live act gigging countrywide and scoring a memorable slot on a Mod all day event with the Purple Hearts at the Ilford Palais. They also had a residency at the Birmingham Barrel Organ and played at the trendy London venue 'Le Beat Route' club.

The band had many line-up changes over the years, but with singer Tony Simpson always fronting the band, and included members that had previously played in local bands The Con Merchants (Jim Fitzpatrick), The Androids (John Groake, and Mike Hancox), Alternative Noize (Pete Shirley Smith), as well as Manchester band The Distractions who signed for T.J.M Records and Factory Records (Tony Trappe, who joined for six gigs). Manager and sometimes keyboards player Martin Frain later formed King Rat, and is currently active in Chomsky Allstars.

Tony Simpson, the bands lead singer remembers:

"In 1979, an ill wind was sweeping through Britain. 'Unemployment' was the ubiquitous headline emblazoned across the national news pages, and in Birmingham, England's second city, a city

241

proud of its industrial heritage, a city that was home to iconic motor brands such as British Leyland, BSA, Rover, Austin and Land Rover, there was an underlying tone of menace, resentment and collective fear; fear that the world of plenty and conservatism was coming to an end."

"Birmingham had long been a melting pot of different races and creeds. In the 1970s, the Irish and West Indian communities filled most of this pot. Co-existence with this community was now under threat from a resurgent National Front and British Movement. People were openly questioning Enoch Powell's right-wing door stepping, which was still fresh in the minds of a susceptible West Midlands voting public."

"Within this miserable framework, a generation of teenagers was now spilling out of a tired education production line. Work apprenticeships had disappeared and the option of enlisting in the army was being taken up by too many. This general malaise was mirrored in the music scene. Birmingham was the spiritual home of the great

British rock band - Robert Plant's Led Zeppelin, Roy Wood's The Move, Ozzy Osborne's Black Sabbath to name just a few. The West Midlands was Rock City, but like the general demise of its manufacturing industry, the metal in the local music was also in need of re casting. Elton John, Cliff Richard, The Sweet and local heroes Slade were all filling a musical void, but none of them were talking or communicating to a generation of teenagers who didn't just want more, they wanted something different."

"They always say you remember where you were when you had your first kiss or first dance, well I remember when I stopped hearing, and started listening. It was The Clash's single 'Tommy Gun', played to me by Ian Richards (soon to become the first member of 021). I was 17, two years older than Ian. When you are that age those things mattered, Ian was plugged into new music way before I was. We would listen to all types of songs; taped music from the BBC's John Peel sessions. Our musical journey took in Crass, The Mekons, The Clash, The Sex Pistols, Dub Reggae, The Fatal

Microbes, and anything on Small Wonder, Fast, or any one of the small independent record labels that were sprouting up all over the UK. DIY was king and as Stiff Little Fingers said, "If we can do it, you can do it too", we thought - hey why not?"

"I was working in the warehouse of a carpet shop; the perfect career for a musician in a garage band. None of us had to worry about further education or careers; these were never on our radar. Kids like us did not go to university."

"Martin Frain lived around the corner from Ian and me. He was the younger brother of Andy, a mutual friend - but it was Martin who caught our attention. Skinny with a keen mind, a sharp wit and a burning sense of justice, Martin would join our regular evenings in Ian's front room as we listened and learned about this new musical landscape that was growing. None of this was happening in isolation. Solihull, our hometown, south of Birmingham, was spawning many groups. We listened in wonder as local band the Swell Maps took radio airplay from David Bowie and Elton John, a feat we found astounding, albeit, on late night BBC Radio 1. Then, other kids we didn't know, but soon would, started to appear on buses, in bright baggy jumpers, spiked hair, monkey boots and tight jeans. In 1979, that look alone singled you out as a Punk, the usual form of Saturday night-out attire being baggy trousers, pastel belts, tight jumpers and penny collars. Like us, the kids on the bus risked both verbal and physical abuse by one and all - the elderly and the young. To be Punk in 1979 mattered, and now at last, so did we."

"I am not really sure how the band started. At first the three of us just looked like we should be a band, Ian in black bondage trousers, ripped multi-layered shirts, often sporting fingerless gloves and smelling of petunia oil, his hair spiky jet black like a hedgehog. Martin, black jeans, bumper boots (baseball boots), always a shirt, usually dark with written words or lines of self-penned lyrics or those by the Clash, dyed blond hair and red neckerchiefs worn around the wrist or neck, and me, tight jeans, tee shirt, my favourites being "F**K Art Lets Dance", or the Clash inspired RAF, Brigade Rosse motif and a black leather jacket. Yep we were a band in waiting, our only issue - we could not play, and aside from Ian's front room drum kit, we had no instruments."

"I had grown up in Shirley an adjoining suburb of Solihull and remembered that I knew one person who had a guitar - Simon Palmer. Palmer was also at school with Martin Frain, although they were not particularly close. He was into Metal and Rock music, a fact we were willing to overlook in exchange for access to his guitar and amp. He brought with him a bass player, named Mark Thomas, equally focused on replicating a musical knowledge that included Hawkwind, Steppenwolf and Led zeppelin. To complete this first improbable line up was Ian Kemp, a halfway house and a musical bridge to Martin, Ian and I. Ian was into Dr Feelgood and T Rex and was to be our rhythm king, he was also a judo partner of Palmers, So far so good. We now had a band but still no name."

"Like many bands of the time we rehearsed and wrote songs before we even considered what we would be called. The feeling was that the name would most likely morph from one of the songs. I wrote the lyrics for our initial songs, and then slowly, Martin would introduce extremely well crafted lyrics in his neat, tidy draughtsman's writing. Martin would soon be fast tracked within his workplace; by all accounts he was a superb draughtsman. Metalrax's loss was to be our gain."

"So how do you choose a name? If I am honest, and I can't remember exactly why, I know that it was me that chose it. I was proud of being from Birmingham, and I figured that our telephone code would identify the band nationally, that was my line of thinking, we had aspirations even then, and it was different too. I suspect we had subconsciously seen 999, but, even now I cannot be sure. So 021 it was. For us the quest was just beginning, now nothing else mattered, not girls, not careers, not money, not Birmingham City Football Club, all we wanted to do was play."

"So on a Friday evening in late April '79 we were ready. Or so we thought. This was to be our first concert. Martin and I had harangued the local high school, Langley, to allow us to headline the end of term show. We were supported by the School punk band The Smarty's, (Ross Fields was the bass player, famous for a shocking red woolly red jumper à la Captain Sensible). They were Ian Richards' school chums, but Ian was now playing with us. The older lads were revelling in the notoriety. All very well and good, but we were still far from tight and certainly not an accomplished musical unit, with a line-up that consisted of me, Tony Simpson, (vocals), Simon Palmer (lead guitar), Ian Kemp, (rhythm guitar), Mark Thomas,(bass guitar) and Ian Richards (drums)."

"After the Smarty's set, and with a mobile disco deck system acting as a PA, borrowed from local DJ Bob Bradshaw, and with us playing under just the DJ's lights, although Mark Thomas was able to secure a strobe, (anything to take the focus off the music), from stage right we entered to play an eclectic set that matched our diverse musical interests. Any concert where you can hear Steppenwolf's 'Born To Be Wild' followed by the Clash's, 'White Riot', with an encore of Iggy Pop's 'I Wanna Be Your Dog' showed the mood of the time and the cross from Progressive Rock to Punk Rock which was taking place across Birmingham."

"The concert was noisy, energetic and eventful; Kemp leapt from the stage bringing down not only his guitar, but his amp and associated sockets with him. I had yet to discover musical keys. I sang "White Riot", first in falsetto and then so low I couldn't reach all the notes, but you know what! We didn't care, we were ecstatic. The crowd fell into three camps, the Smarty's fans hated us, the general school population couldn't wait for the disco to resume or were indifferent, and the rest - our friends, family and assorted girlfriends were overprotective and would have clapped if we had blown a fuse. We were now truly up and running though, and for many of the following gigs, achieved the same audience reaction. 1979 was certainly going to be a long learning curve!"

"Having played the sum total of one concert, the last thing we expected is what happened next. Martin arrived at my house one evening to tell me that if we could raise the cash, we could appear on an E.P with Mass Media, a band whose members I knew from Solihull Tech - Martin Hughes and soon-to-be Pinkies' guitarist Mark Young. Now Mass Media had already played in the final of the Melody Makers' Battle of the Bands and did very well; winning the Midlands' sector. They looked fantastic – think Echo and the Bunnymen - and were much cooler than we were on the local music scene. Martin and his then girlfriend Ann Spelman were two of those original punks we had seen on the bus."

"Of course we reply immediately to Paul Panic of The Accused stating that we will not only join the E.P, but in our own shy way, would like to have track one side two, if they are having track one side one. The original E.P line-up is set; from

250

memory, Rankin Roger's Dum Dum Boys, The Accused, Mass Media and 021. Of course this didn't actually materialise. Both other bands drop out, leaving the Accused and 021. So what do we do? Martin had heard rumours of a band from Sheldon called the Undertakers and approached them to see if they would join in. Paul then secured, via the common room at Solihull Technical College, the Cracked Actors, like us months old, but still yet to perform live."

"So after much wrangling, saving my weekly salary from the carpet shop and finally handing over our share of the cash to Paul, we arrive at Frank Skarth 4 track Recording Studios for what we had thought would be a forty minute session - three minutes to run through the song, three to play and then half an hour to mix. At the time this was what we believed in, and is, in many ways the essence of the E.P. I remember the session, the drums were recorded separately, then each track overlaid, finally I put over a voice track. I am not sure I even bothered to listen to the full playback and we certainly did not hear the track again until it was actually pressed onto vinyl. But we had all underestimated how much it would cost, and at the end of the session we weren't allowed to leave until we emptied out our pockets. Clearly we did not have enough to purchase a master tape of our own from the afternoon's work."

"To pass the time away while the other bands were in the studio we took hold of the house phone, (we were certainly not in a dedicated studio, just a normal suburban house) and started to bump the dial. This consisted of tapping the tone dials repeatedly until you had your number. As I remember we spent time with members of The Accused and Cracked Actors, whose track seemed extremely professional and presentable compared to ours. I can't remember getting home but I am told we left the other bands to pay. If this is true, I apologise; we really were that arrogant."

"Paul Panic was now turning into Solihull's version of Malcolm McLaren in league with Martin Frain's,

Bernie Rhodes. They had secured the Solihull Civic Hall and we were now to support the E.P with a live concert featuring the four bands. This was clearly a step up for us from Langley School, to play at one of the biggest live venues in South Birmingham."

"Here is my other musical milestone. I have already mentioned that The Clash and 'Tommy Gun' made me sit up and listen, well on a bright Saturday morning, Martin and I made the three mile trip to Paul Panic's house. Although not a close friend, Paul attended the same high school as me, as did Colin from G.B.H. He lived a stone's throw away from Light Hall School in Shirley, so I joined Martin for the drive over. We collected 10 boxes of 25 records each, and headed back to my place, my record player was waiting; the pair of us discussing the ease in which we have entered the music industry."

"And then it happens, we listen first to The Accused, followed by the Cracked Actors, and then the first strains of our track 'Robot' are played on side two and my heart sinks. This is just awful; dropped notes and non- existent mix. I am crestfallen, I don't say anything to Martin, we know we have let ourselves down and the hype around the E.P has been extensive. Just when we think it can't get any worse, the first chords of the Undertakers track 'Illusions' strike, it's magnificent, competent, clear and catchy, it is at that moment, that our rivalry begins. If we can't beat them musically, we will certainly make sure we are the best known and most popular. All of this is compounded by the fact that they hail from Sheldon and we are from Olton and Shirley, two tribal opposites in Solihull, both with vociferous followings not unknown to the Police."

"The weeks leading up to the concert became a major marketing pitch. We were all promoting and selling tickets, posters got put up on the notice boards in the local sixth form college as well as Solihull Tech. This was still a very local affair and 021 had yet to spread their collective wings and seek true musical competence. However we are fuelled by a desire to play and perform three minute wonders and write more tracks and start to believe in ourselves. Always at the back of my mind I knew that we were just a rock band with two punks, but now was not the time to change that. We needed to play and not let ourselves down again. Martin wrote to the local paper and we appeared on a half page, holding the record's D.I.Y cover in front of a red telephone box at the top end of my road. All set then for the big gig, hundreds of teenagers turn up, unfortunately so do the gangs."

"There have been many varying accounts of this night told by people present, so I will not repeat them all, but from my point of view this is what happened:"

"The Accused were, as organisers, going to headline, with The Undertakers taking the penultimate spot. That left us or the Cracked Actors to start the show. Now for us this was totally unacceptable. Why? Because we had sold the most tickets and brought a large contingent from Shirley with us, many of whom would not arrive until after the first acts had played, as they would still be in the local pubs, The Undertakers had also brought a sizeable following from Hobbs Moat/ Sheldon who were, unfortunately for the Accused and Cracked Actors, of the same mind."

"As I recall, we went missing, to the 'Captain's Locker', a well known town centre pub, and at the time, the place where the local punks hung out. When we returned later I was feeling slightly nervous, trying to act cool as it dawned on me that I had never performed in front of over 400 people before. We eventually took to the stage and after playing half our set, all hell breaks loose. I can't remember if we were last on or not, what I do remember is, fan's having running battles across the stage, musical equipment being used as weapons and the Shirley/Sheldon rivalry rapidly having turned into an Undertaker's versus 021 issue. Now in truth we had no beef with them, we didn't like some of their badges and stickers, but respected them as a band and did attend as many of their gigs, as they themselves would later attend ours."

"During this period, many other bands were striking out from Solihull: Spizz Energi, The Cult Figures, A Mental Block, and Swell Maps. All of us knew each other and played together at some time or on the same bill."

"After the Civic Hall gig, both Simon and Mark moved on. I think the experience of two gigs and a record in three months was enough for them. For the rest of us, it provided the opportunity to really kick on and show the world what we could do."

"We went through a major shift in focus and line-up during 1980.Both Martin and I felt the desire to pen and deliver three minute pieces of power and pace. We advertised for both a bass player and guitarist of renown and repute. We held auditions at rehearsal rooms in Wake Green Road's Motor City Rhythm's (MCR) Rehearsal Studio's. Sessions often overseen by David Snead and Steve Riddle, the later would later move to the Virgin Mobile facility. We were now also supported by a full time driver, Mark, A.K.A Frankie, who was a plumber by day, but for gigs, allowed us access to his big bright orange van. Mark was a friend of Ian Kemp's and Martin Frain's, he was also a big music fan and a regular at the Golden Lion (A.K.A Lords, A.K.A The Lair) in Solihull, a pub fast becoming the town's new punk hang out and local gig venue."

"It was at MCR studio's on a Saturday afternoon that Vivian Elmore walked into the rehearsal studio, he said very little, listened to our tracks then played them all, straight off the bat, better and sharper than we had ever heard them. Martin and I just looked at each other; Yeah, O.K, you wanna join? OK, we have a gig next week at the Golden Lion, Solihull; see you there at 6pm, on stage at 8pm. And that is really how this most amazing guitarist and songwriter came into our lives. He looked like a Ramone and played like anyone he wanted to be. Ian Kemp literally met Viv on stage. For 021, a legend was born. A week later we went back to MCR and recorded 'Jealousy', 'Whatever Happened to You' and 'Images', a track later included on the 'A Tale of two cities' album that Paul Panic released, with Elmore playing all instruments bar rhythm guitar. Now we were truly on our way."

"Before Elmore joined we had experimented with many different people, some rejecting us, others rejected by us. Mike Hogan of the Undertakers recorded a definitive version of 'Heaven and Hell', a song he wrote with Frain. Ross Field from the Smarty's played on 'Fashion Addicts', an early track. More significantly, Jimmy Fitzpatrick, a wonderful, if spectacularly unreliable bass player we stole from Birmingham band Con Merchants, played a version of 'Help me make it through the Night' which was always a real crowd pleaser."

"The line-up of Elmore, Fitzpatrick, Richards, Kemp and myself played gigs further afield and on the same bill as The Beat, Blurt, the Au Pairs, UB40, the Denizens, as well as taking part in the famous 'Lark in the Park' music festival at Cannon Hill

Park in Birmingham, where we played in front of a crowd of soldiers and included a cover version of Stiff Little Finger's 'Wasted Youth' in our set!."

"In 1980 along with The Undertakers, Helpless Huw, and others, we played a concert at Weymouth Pavilion. This was once again organised by Paul Panic of the Accused. We were now gigging regularly in the Midlands, with a residency at the Golden Lion, Solihull, and supporting concerts at the Golden Eagle, Barrel Organ, and Kit Kat club amongst others. Ian Kemp, a popular and integral part of the initial band, was forced to make a choice; a career in the fire service or to chase the dream. We missed Ian after he left the band. In later years I have seen him featured in the press as a senior fire officer so who knows? For him maybe it was the right call."

"The final pieces of the jigsaw were being put together; in late 1980, Mike Hancox (bass) joined the band, followed swiftly by John Groake (drums) - both from Birmingham ska -punk band, the Androids (hear them on Last FM). It was at this point that the band finally had the musical balance to reach its zenith."

"We now had a solid rhythm section that was being driven forward by Elmore's song writing skills. Looking back I can see that we wrote many of our finest pieces during this period, rehearsing three times a week in an egg carton encrusted room above Garrett's second-hand shop on the Stratford Road, in Camp Hill, Birmingham. All this feverish energy and rehearsing, produced a new and unique Power-Mod sound, prompting the need for regular gigs and a desire to firmly establish ourselves across the Midlands. During this period we headlined regularly at the Golden Eagle, Hill Street, the Barrel Organ, Digbeth, and Moseley's Fighting Cocks. Some of the Androids followers were now also starting to attend our gigs, the attire of the crowd changing from Punk to Mod and Soul boy. Mike Hancox bought a love of soul and John Groarke bought a Mod pace to many of our tunes."

"As we were not gigging as much as we would have liked, we started to record, notably going into Rich bitch Studios in Selly Oak Birmingham where in one weekly session we recorded many of the tracks that would eventually appear on the Mell Square Musick the Album c.d. One of our most accomplished recordings was 'Simple Minds', a 16 track version of what had been a popular live song, written by Frain and Fitzpatrick a year earlier, The track is sadly ruined by vocals which are at best stretched, and an octave higher than they really needed to be, I distinctly remember arriving into the studio one afternoon and emerging 24 hours later into a snow shrouded Birmingham city centre, clutching desk tapes of not only Simple Minds, but, 'Must be Love', another track yet to see the digital light of day."

"And so it was, on a miserable grey Saturday in February 1981 we drove up to M.R.S Studios in Walsall, to record what would become our next single, 'The Pop Song', we had a clear idea as to the sound we wanted, and the session engineer and studio owner, John Taylor, played no small part in ensuring we got what we set out to achieve."

"We were constantly marketing ourselves, sending letters and making phone calls from local public telephone boxes; word of mouth had resulted in an invite for us to play at a Mod All-dayer at the Ilford Palais, supporting the Purple Hearts. Various demo recording sessions took place during 1981 and 1982 and finally, in September of that year, we released 'The Pop Song' on our own - UK Pop Records label. To support the single, we managed to negotiate a monthly residency at the Barrel Organ in Birmingham, its central location, aligned with a vigorous poster and a well-documented graffiti campaign (which saw a huge picture of our name emblazoned on the front page of the 'Birmingham Evening Mail', under the Headline – 'Clear the Filth off Birmingham's walls') it greatly helped reinforce our following with the local Mod and Scooter Scene."

"Late in 1982 we were invited to play at 'Le Beat Route' club in Greek Street, Soho, and the Moonlight club in West Hampstead. A week later we were back in London, and as Martin and I walked down Carnaby Street, I saw not only 021 badges on sale, but also small picture post cards with me wearing a cycle shirt, taken on stage from the previous all dayer at the Palais."

"Solihull, The Undertakers and our punk roots seemed a long way off, but we were driven by a fear of failure and the acceptance of a life less ordinary, I was still working at Allied Carpets by day, earning enough to pay for rehearsals and equipment, but it was horrible and soul destroying, but I firmly believed that not only were we going to 'make it' but that we would with some aplomb."

"As the year progressed, so did public interest in the band and week after week the Barrel Organ was packed to overflowing, with scooters parked all around the block. This modicum of success, however, was the beginning of the end, a small fracas between some of our mod fans and local rude boys ended up in a full scale riot on Digbeth High Street, unfortunately, right outside the police station! The result, we were banned from playing in Birmingham; of course now in hind sight, this was fantastic publicity, and by now our single had achieved limited evening BBC Radio 1 airplay as well, but with many of the clubs and bars that supported us now closed, we were running out of energy and more importantly suitable venues to play."

"During the early 80's we were one of many, many bands that made up a cultural and uniquely British musical landscape, providing a musical heritage and back drop for those that followed. In the late 90's 'the Pop song' was sampled by 'Future Sound of London', a further twist that saw the single take on a life of its own. It became sought after by record collectors across four continents in the late 1990's, and was heavily bootlegged on various compilation albums. It is the opening track on the 'Power Poppers' album volume 1, released by welsh label 'On the Run

Records' the album cover actually being a version of 'The Pop Song' single's artwork."

"In the early 2000's it had established itself on internet power pop radio, and is now widely acknowledged as a classic of the early eighties Mod Scene. If you own an original mint copy, you will not get much change from $200. I have the original recording receipt and can confirm it cost considerably less than that to record. But how do you put a value on the magic of the moment."

Tony Simpson – Lead Singer of 021

23/. WE'VE GOT THAT SINKING FEELING

After the Weymouth experience that the band itself never had, The Accused never played again live. We planned to get some more support gigs with our 'Dexy's' connections, but what happened next basically broke the band up.

The following month 'Dexy's' were playing two shows in Birmingham, back to back, the first was on July 17th 1980 at Gay Tower Ballroom and this was to be followed the next day, by a special under 18's show at the Cedar Club. Somehow their drummer's hi hat cymbal and stand had gone missing after the previous night's show in Liverpool, and Simon, our drummer who we had forgiven after his no show at Weymouth, was surprised to receive a call late at night from 'Dexy's' manager Dave Corke asking if they could borrow his cymbals for the next two days.

Dave wanted Simon to get down to the venue immediately to leave his equipment there; well Simon was concerned about leaving the cymbals that actually belonged to his brother Mark, unattended overnight, and he was certainly not best pleased to have been phoned up at ten o'clock in the evening, and consequently raised some objections, which resulted in a certain 'Foxtrot Oscar!' being uttered. This led to an irate manager of Dexy's Midnight Runners telling Simon in no uncertain terms that he wouldn't be helping us again, or getting us any more gigs in the future.

When Martin and I found out, we at first went mad, blaming Simon for ruining the bands chances. This was effectively when we all split up. We drifted apart for a while, but despite everything that had happened, the bonds remained strong, and we eventually saw things Simon's way, and didn't blame him at all.

Martin Hope and 'Ed' Eccles then formed a short lived bedroom band called Zippzed, rehearsing old Zits songs, and writing some new ones too. Simon still had his Vespa and was well into his scooter rallies, the new mod revival scene, and the burgeoning Two Tone movement.

My old school friend David Coombs and I, had started listening to a midlands band called The Photo's around this time, after having seen them perform live at the Fighting Cocks pub in Moseley, Birmingham. Led by Wendy Wu, they were a phenomenal live band, who had, pre Wendy, been a punk band called Satan's Rats. Knowing that it would be ages till they played again in Birmingham, we looked at their tour dates in 'Sounds' music paper and decided to hitch-hike up to Middleton, a suburb of Manchester to see them play live again. We did eventually get a couple of lifts, standing by the side of Spaghetti Junction in Birmingham, holding our cardboard destination signs, but by the time we arrived and located the venue, we were shocked to find out that the gig had been cancelled. To add to the misery it had now started to rain. We couldn't be bothered to try for a lift home that evening, and so bought some beer and spent an uncomfortable night like a pair of tramps on a couple of benches in Middleton Park.

Martin and I still really wanted The Accused to continue, and so we had a get together in September, primarily to discuss how to get rid of the pile of unsold records residing under my bed. We decided to put another advert in the music press, this time, in the 'New Musical Express'. The advert appeared in the back of the paper on October 4th 1980, the price being raised to 70p a copy to allow for the postage costs.

Over a few beers we thought it might be funny to send a copy to Prince Andrew at Buckingham Palace. We kind of suspected it was a wasted stamp, but to our surprise on the 21st November a letter arrived in my letterbox from London on Palace headed paper, saying that His Royal Highness had asked the Royal office to return it to us, as he was aware of how much these things cost to produce and was sure we would like to use his copy for further promotion! It also said that he wasn't able to comment on the quality of the recordings as the danger existed that opinions of the Royal Family could be used for commercial purposes. I wonder if he played it to his brother, as it wouldn't be very long before Prince Charles was to be financing our next project.

Meanwhile my school mates, the two Dave's, Trevor and I embarked on a week's holiday on a boat on the River Thames. We had hired a boat from Blake's, a very well respected boatyard, and took turns negotiating the various locks, which proved to be surprisingly easy when we were sober, but by the time the beer was loaded aboard at the first town, and the first cans opened, it soon became a surreal experience.

It became abundantly clear that a boat took quite a while to actually stop when we needed it too, nonetheless, we had a brilliant time mooring up in Reading and visiting the tiny 'Target Club' to watch a local band perform, they were called El Seven. We even spotted the Hexagon Centre, where the snooker on television was broadcast from.

Having moored up in a small place called Goring one night, we set off to find a country pub, which was so quiet, we soon left again, we sat up most of the night on the top of the boat drinking and singing a song we had made up 'It's so boring in Goring'.

Trevor had actually brought an air rifle with him, and the rest of us had high power catapults, and so we were soon causing terror on the waterways, shooting at apples floating in the water. However we soon discovered people on the other boats, had assumed we were firing at ducks and must have informed the authorities, we soon became marked men. The word had been sent out to various lock keepers to keep a close eye on our activities. The beer kept on flowing, and one night on the way to Maidenhead we moored up somewhere, and got very drunk indeed. I have vague memories of being put into the recovery position, after dying my hair orange, jumping into the river and lamenting Sid Vicious' loss to the world of punk.

The nice couple from the boat moored up behind us must have heard the commotion and come to help, I was later told their faces were a picture after coming aboard and passing a huge pile of 'men's' magazines we had purchased in a sale for ten pence each, an air rifle, crates of beer, and blood (or was it hair dye?) all over the floor. The next

271

morning however, hangovers aside, all was well, until one of the Dave's, attempting a three point turn in a backwater, realised the boat wasn't going to stop as quickly as he would have liked.

The resultant cracking sound of fibre glass was heard by us all, we watched helplessly, as the small boat we had hit, very quickly started to sink below the water line. Luckily there wasn't anyone around, and in some haste we got the hell out of there, as soon as we could, full speed ahead. We resolved to take things a little calmer from then on, but on our final night afloat, the beer and cider were once again flowing freely; it wasn't long before a failed attempt to enter the cabin graciously from the boat's roof, resulted in the galley window being smashed.

The following morning, we cruised into the boatyard to face up to the consequences and the bill for all the damages, very apologetically and out of pocket once more, but oh the memories, and oh the laughs we had recalling it all, on the car journey home.

Around this time, Lorraine and I were still finalising the 'Tale of 2 Cities' album and decided that because some of the bands on it were so good, it might be worth playing some of their songs to the London based record labels.

We then spotted in the Birmingham Evening Mail that the 'Prince Charles Trust' was offering grants to young people's projects that they deemed worthwhile.

What could be more worthwhile, than an album of local talent with sixteen bands, involving around sixty people? We put a letter together and eagerly awaited a reply, which to our surprise wasn't long in arriving. They were indeed interested, and wanted to send someone to my house to talk to us. Of course we joked about how it would be funny if the Prince himself turned up! The meeting went well and they seemed very impressed, and before we knew it, we had a 300 pound cheque sent to us to help towards putting the album together.

Off we went, Lorraine and I, to London, in February 1981 and first rented a small room in a bed and breakfast called 'Abba House' in South Kensington, for a few days. We talked ourselves into record companies by day, playing them the best of the bands recordings from the album. Actually the first time we went down on the train to London we had planned on renting a flat in Brixton, but when we arrived, the landlady claimed she hadn't received our deposit cheque and wouldn't let us stay. As it was getting late, we caught a tube back to Euston and planned to sit on the station all night. Eventually it got too much and we found a hotel along Euston Road and persuaded the night porter to sell us a cup of tea. We couldn't afford a room but he took pity on us and let us rest for a few hours in a lounge room just off the reception area.

We would change our paper money in the banks for bags of ten pence pieces and find two red phone boxes situated next to each other, where we would proceed to ring up all the labels we could think of, and basically tell them they had to see us, as we were about to go home to consider offers from their rivals. It pretty much worked every time as they all thought they might be missing out on something. It was strange, but exciting, to be in the capital suddenly entering into the world of the major labels, walking up E.M.I's famous staircase in Manchester Square, looking at all the gold discs on their walls, and letting our imaginations run away with us.

That was to be the first of three visits to London, as we returned again in March and July with more tapes, and rented rooms in Fulham and Catford to spread the word. We also used our time in London to enter a couple of Studio's to get the individual master tapes spliced together to create the album; first stop was at Stage One Studio's in Forest Gate (I remember 'The The' were recording their single 'Cold Spell Ahead' there at the time) and later at 'Y' Studios in central London which was a very plush facility set up in the Y.M.C.A building .We soon had a finished version of the album spliced together and equalised onto a reel of ¼ inch Ampex tape.

In January 1981, the newspapers had been full of the arrest of the Yorkshire Ripper, Peter Sutcliffe, ending his reign of terror across northern England, but by the time we reached Catford in July, there was rioting on the streets of nearby Lewisham. We would sit in the little rented flat at night listening to the Police and Fire sirens, whilst looking out of the windows at the plumes of smoke and the glow of the fires in the distance. On Sunday July 5th I decided to introduce Lorraine to the joys of punk, she was a huge David Bowie fan and wasn't too enthusiastic about an evening in the company of The Damned, Anti Nowhere League, Ruts DC, and Vice Squad at the Lyceum Theatre, just off the Strand in the West End. On arrival there was a huge crowd of punks waiting to get in, pushing and shoving; the crowd surged and Lorraine narrowly avoided getting seriously hurt by shards of glass from a poster display window that got smashed in the crush. The gig itself degenerated into a trading of insults, between bands and audience, of a kind certainly never to be witnessed at a Bowie gig!

We had used the Prince's Trust money to pay for the rent of accommodation and travel costs, whilst playing the band's tapes to record labels, and we managed to get appointments at all of the majors and most of the important independent labels over that summer of 1981. The reaction was somewhat mixed, but a couple of bands, namely Human Cabbages from Coventry and Ideal Husbands from Shipston on Stour usually got the best response. This led to further meetings being set up, but nothing much followed. We sort of knew we would have to release the album ourselves, which was fine, but we were running out of money fast, and so had to return to Birmingham to assess the best way forward. On July 29th Prince Charles and Lady Diana got married in St Paul's Cathedral, watched by 750 million people, the largest television audience in history. We didn't know at the time that we were soon to be meeting the prince ourselves.

Within a few weeks of returning from London, I received a letter saying that Prince Charles had requested meeting some of the people his trust had helped, and inviting Lorraine and I to meet him personally and present the finished album to him on October 14th at the Oakland's

Community Centre in Handsworth. This was of course an honour but there was one huge problem; the album only existed on a reel to reel spool of tape!

We realised that the best that we could do in the time left before his visit, was to get some cassettes made up, I phoned a few people and asked Max from one of the bands on the album, 'The Solicitors', who I knew to be talented in the art department, to design a sleeve. He came up with a sort of new romantically styled cover adapted from an image in Jean Cocteau's film 'Orphee' from 1950. This was actually the same image that The Smith's would later use in 1983, for the cover of their debut single 'This Charming man'. We got around 50 copies duplicated for the day and set them up as a display on a trestle table in a large hall in the Community centre.

There were around fifty people present and around another fifty heavy looking security people, trying to look discreet. We recognised David Hinds from reggae band Steel Pulse with his amazing dreadlocked hair, and waited patiently for the Prince's arrival. His helicopter landed on a nearby football field and after around ten minutes chatting to the large crowd outside, he entered the hall and started talking to the various dignitaries. Lorraine and I were thinking about how we were going to talk to him about Human

Cabbages and Sadists, Undertakers and The Accused, but in retrospect maybe we should have perhaps discussed 'Ideal Husbands!!'

When he approached our little table with just a few cassettes scattered on it, I thought he looked a little surprised, but after shaking our hands, and Lorraine curtseying for probably the only time in her life, he turned out to be a pleasure to talk to, and seemed to take a real interest in the bands we had managed to bring together and the album in general. A day like no other and now we had officially got the royal seal of approval; he didn't seem to want to buy a copy though!

The resulting album stands as a snapshot of what was happening in the small pubs and clubs of Birmingham and Coventry in 1981, and shows that although the punk bands were still as strong as ever, there were also new ideas and rhythms being tried, with a few synthesisers creeping in too. The overall impression left, listening to the album today, to my ears, is of the sheer quality of song writing that was coming through, with boundless energy and enthusiasm by these bands with nothing to lose and everything to gain.

24/. X TREME DREAMS AND KWOIRS

One of the bands from the album that Lorraine and I had high hopes for, were a five piece called Dream Sequence. They had previously existed briefly as a far more punk sounding band called Hygiene, who used to wear dentists tops and had only managed to record one three song demo. However, now they had evolved into something, really rather special. We had first spotted them playing at Solihull Civic Hall back in February 1981. The five members undoubtedly took a lot of influence from bands like Joy Division and early Magazine, but their singer Steve Bill had a really haunting, and at the same time, quite creepy voice. It drew the listener in, and got you totally hooked; it was like you were the only person that would learn a secret that he wanted to share with you. Steve dressed in old fashioned clothing both on and off stage, and drove a grey Ford Popular 103E, it was his pride and joy, until one day he parked it outside Lorraine's parent's house and it got hit by another car, he took the news like a death in his family, but very soon replaced it with an identical one but this time in black.

Very early on in their career the band had made a video presentation of four of their songs complete with silent film style subtitle boards, introducing each track, and dramatic lighting effects. These mini films Lorraine and I had taken to London on the professional 'U-Matic' video format, thinking how impressive it would look, only to find out that almost no one had the correct machine to play them on. We signed them to a management contract; they changed the band name to 'Die La Kwoir' and recorded some great tracks like 'Ha Ha April Fool' and 'Death in a Darkroom'. We set up some shows for them in July and August at the Opposite Lock Club in Birmingham and at 'Lords' at The Golden Lion in Solihull. Matt Copplestone, the band's lighting engineer, had previously worked as a technician for The Undertakers, and was affectionately known to them as 'Matt the Money', but that is another story!

When they played live around Birmingham and Solihull, they actually built scenery that recreated a living room on the stage, complete with windows, chairs and old fashioned lamp standards. The band sound was led by menacing bass guitar from Kevin Galloway, and attacking synth sounds from D James B, a.k.a, David Bates, all the time being driven from the back by a drummer simply known as 'Craig' (Morrissey). Steve meanwhile was always the main centre of attention, holding maniac stares with the crowd, whilst adding guitar to the mix in carefully measured doses. The fifth original member was guitarist Jeff; when Lorraine suggested his hair was too long and that he needed to change his image, the band simply sacked him the very next day.

Totally out of character really, but one day we all drove to London, after purchasing lots of cans of spray string, and thinking we might create some publicity, we turned up at the weekly music paper 'Sounds' and covered the poor receptionist in it, from head to toe. Nothing ever appeared in the paper, but then again we may have even forgotten to leave a tape in all the excitement.

Lorraine went on to work with the band for many years after my involvement stopped, and eventually fronted a band with some of the surviving members of Die La Kwoir, calling themselves firstly, 'Tanzshau' then 'Monkey Messiah' and finally 'The Jetsons'.

Ironically, years later it was the previously sacked Jeff who Lorraine fell in love with, and eventually married. All three bands with Lorraine singing, released some fine singles and the member's signed a publishing deal with a top London company. The band played some great live shows in both

Birmingham and London, and Lorraine proved beyond doubt, that she has a very strong and totally unique singing voice. However this was in the future, back in 1981, I was wondering what to do next.

Incidentally if anyone reading this knows the whereabouts of the Die La Kwoir video tapes please get in touch as it would be nice to make them available, especially as two of the members singer Steve Bill, and bass player Kevin Galloway have since sadly died.

Kevin   Steve

25/. Y NOT TRY AGAIN, IT'S SHELLSHOCK AND BLOOD RARE LION

While Lorraine was busy managing Die La Kwoir, I was now helping 'The Solicitor's' out, and Max Body, their singer, had taken the D.J. slot on Monday nights at a city centre club called Sloopys. It was a small basement club in Corporation Street, Birmingham, with a great sound system, and we both took turns on the twin decks playing all the latest, interesting and obscure records that we both owned. Then we hit on the idea of putting a few bands on as well, to bring in the crowd. I asked The Undertakers to play one Monday in November, but by this time they had changed the name of the band to Me-I-Mafia; the same line up, but introducing a more reggae based sound to their music.

I was also rehearsing again with Simon Baker and our original 'Accused' guitarist Dave Browne; we would get together in my bedroom at home in Shirley, and 'jam' out song ideas, writing quickly, we found ourselves penning a full set of new songs in just over a couple of weeks. Titles such as 'War song', 'Private hell', and 'Bayonet stuck in my heart', cemented our anti-war stance and complimented our customised army clothing. We named the band Shellshock, and I booked our first and as it turned out, only gig, supporting Me-I-Mafia, at that aforementioned gig at Sloopys. We decided not to have a bass player as we wanted it to sound abrasive and hard hitting. The gig was a great success but for some reason I can't remember, we didn't pursue the band further.

The next project, the following year in 1982 was, at first, just Dave Browne and myself; Blood Rare Lion was the name of the band. I had written a song previously called 'Rare Lion' (an anagram of Lorraine); it was a song of loss and sorrow, but with a happy ending of breaking free from the chains of everyday life. We went into a local recording studio near to where Lorraine still lived with her parents, in Castle Bromwich called 'Fairmorn Studio's' and recorded the track with a drum machine backing us. The result was so good we decided to form a band adding a third member Rod Thompson, and decided to make a video of the song. We asked the local paper to put out an appeal for anyone who would like to appear in it; just send a photo and contact details. We were astonished to receive lots of letters, full of photographs of all sorts of assorted oddballs, and even some normal people too! However again, the whole idea soon fell apart, the proposed video never got made and we were left with just the one song recorded.

At the age of twenty and with my sister Sue now legally able to drink, we, along with our respective friends often found ourselves in Solihull Town Centre, at the weekends in 'The Captain's Locker', or the 'Snooty Fox' public houses. The other bands from college drank there too, and each weekend was spent talking about music and meeting new friends. During that summer of '82 with our parents away on holiday, Sue and I held a couple of after pub parties back at our house. Fuelled by my dad's home-made wine they became nights of legend. At one of them I met a girl looking very ill, having had too much to drink, she was collapsed on the upstairs landing and her name I soon learned was Sarah. She became my first long term girlfriend. During the next six years we were both to enjoy our fifteen minutes of fame, and more beside; but I'm jumping ahead. The following is a year by year account of the adventures of a band that released one single, had one song released on a compilation album, appeared on national television and radio, got featured in the national and local press and even appeared on the national ITV News at 5.45 after paying a visit to number 10 Downing Street, it sure was fun while it lasted.........

26/. ZEITGEIST, THE EYE DO IT YEARS AND BEYOND

Sarah and her school friend's had formed a gang, calling themselves 'The Squad', who were all fans of The Undertakers, she had previously been the girlfriend of guitarist, Paul Hughes, another member Caroline went on to marry the bass player Mike Hogan.. We got on well and she mentioned that she wanted to be a singer, and so we decided to try to start a band. Martin Hope who I hadn't heard from for a while called one night and I talked him into joining. Sarah wanted another friend, Debbie Craig, known at that time as 'Lucas', due to her hair being the same colour as the 'Lucozade' drink (dark orange) to join too. We asked a mate of Martin's, Andy Foxall to come in on guitar, and he adopted the name, 'Blind Pugh', I have no idea why! We briefly had a keyboards player called Marko but no one now seems to remember who he was; he obviously made a big impression!

One day in the post an invitation arrived from the authors, B George and Martha De Foe, who had compiled a punk/new-wave listings book called 'Volume-The International Discography of the New Wave', telling me that the Mell Square Musick E.P was featured within its pages. The letter included some free tickets for its English launch party at Heaven night club in London on Halloween night October 31$^{st.}$ There were to be two bands playing live as well –Virgin Prunes and S.P.K.

With our new band now named Eye Do It, taking shape, we thought it would be good to print up some flyers and hand them out at the club on the night. They read 'Eye Do It - the sound you'll see in '83'. We all travelled down in a rented mini bus, dressed up in Halloween costumes; Debbie had even acquired a real shroud from a friend who worked in a mortuary and proceeded to get morbidly drunk. We handed out the flyers to let the Londoners know what to expect in the New Year.

The mystery man Marko didn't work out and Lucas left the band after only a few rehearsals, we then placed adverts for a new keyboards player in the music press and local papers, and by March '83 we were recording our first demo tape at Boyling Point Studio's in Birmingham with engineer John O'Boyle, and 'Red' (Sarah's new name, as it was her favourite colour) became the lead singer. Our new keyboard player was a girl who responded to the advert called Soraya Kahn. Three songs were recorded namely, 'The Well', 'Wax', and 'Stop Don't feel'. Sarah, 'Red' was proving herself to be a very inventive lyricist, her subject matter was often very deep and mysterious, but although we often didn't know what the songs were about, it all fitted together well.

We then added a percussionist, Rachel Cox, and sacked Soraya for being unreliable. I can remember us having a band meeting and formulating an ambitious plan to get the band onto television within three months; but how were we going to achieve that?

By now Andy had left and in came Dave Browne who had now changed his name to Charlie E, after the famous baseball player, and had taken to wearing baseball clothing and wielding a bat. Then one day he rang me up all excited and said that he thought he could put an electric pick up into the bat and turn it into a one string guitar! Here was our television news angle, and with the strange instrument now made and actually working, we contacted the local T.V stations with our unusual story. We almost got them interested too, but at the last minute they dropped our piece from the broadcast.

By now we had started rehearsing regularly at both 'Diamond Sound Studio's' and 'Concert Lighting' which was an underground rehearsal complex in Birmingham city centre. On April 16th we played our first gig at the Star Club and on June 4th we were featured on the same poster as The Smiths, who were just embarking on their first U.K tour and playing at the Fighting Cocks pub in Moseley, just prior to our gig there. We also contacted the band Punishment of Luxury who promised us some support slots which never materialised, then after more gigs at The Mermaid pub in Sparkbrook on June 30th, and the newly opened 'Duma Express venue' at the Opposite Lock club in the city centre on July 14th, we secured a support slot with the punk band 'Serious Drinking' at 'The Golden Eagle' in Hill Street, Birmingham on July 18th; this was to be our big break, but right at the last minute it got cancelled. Just as well really, we were more of an alternative pop band than a punk band.

However still looking for a newsworthy story to promote the band, Dave told us that he had overheard someone in a pub talking about a new Government Initiative called the 'Enterprise Allowance Scheme', which allowed people to formulate new business ideas and get paid forty pounds a week each for a period of a year, to turn the said ideas into a viable business. Bingo we thought; if we could talk them into allowing a band to apply, we could sign off the dole and become professional musicians and get paid for it as well.

We duly applied and attended some business seminars at the local Chamber of Commerce. We set up a meeting with Sarah's father Ken, and he agreed to finance our first record release. This was to be issued on my own 'No Rip off Records' label with national distribution handled by 'Nine Mile and the Cartel', who at the time, were the U.K's largest independent record distribution network. Sarah's sister Carole would design the sleeve, with some extra input from the members of the band, incorporating Egyptian hieroglyphs, spelling out our respective initials. Carole was and I'm sure still is, a very talented designer/artist with a very sharp sense of style.

We hired out a small, but highly recommended recording studio called 'The Attic' with its Engineer/owner Jon Buxton to demo the tracks and then moved on to F.S.R Studio's to record the actual record. Frank Skarth who had engineered the Mell Square Musick E.P, had now opened this plush new 24 track recording studio just outside Birmingham city centre, and we booked a week long session to record the single's two songs. The 'A' side was to be, 'Stop Don't Feel' and the B side, a new song 'Hold Back'.

Martin had now purchased an electronic drum kit but as he couldn't afford the industry standard 'Simmons' kit yet, had purchased a cheap and nasty copy kit with triangular plastic pads. My lasting memories of that kit was that he had to carry around a soldering iron with him at all times, as usually with just a few hits, all the wires and electronics would shake loose.

The first three days of the recording session were taken up with trying very hard, against the limitations of this cheap drum kit, to come up with a useable drum sound to commit to tape. This as it turned out was to prove very useful spare time for the rest of the band. We entered F.S.R Studio's on August 22nd 1983 to start our week of recording. Just three days earlier we had officially started our year on the 'Enterprise Allowance Scheme', having been accepted just a few weeks earlier. We were just pleased to be able to sign off the dole and try our hands at being professional musicians; we thought no more of it really.

However on our very first morning in the studio the Birmingham Post newspaper printed a small piece mentioning that Eye Do It had become the first ever Government sponsored rock band; it was news to us!

All of a sudden we started receiving calls from newspapers and news agencies asking for interviews and comments. No sooner had we put the phone down, it would start ringing again, and we slowly realised we were fast becoming a big news story. The following day the Birmingham Evening Mail sent a reporter and photographer round to the studio, and a freelance reporter called to say he could sell our story to the nationals. The next day a BBC reporter came down to record an interview with us, that was to be aired across 44 BBC local radio stations, this was getting silly! and all this with Frank Skarth still busy trying to get a decent drum sound out of Martin's kit; at first he thought we were winding him up about all the sudden interest in the band, but soon he realised it was true, as it was he who had to keep interrupting the session to answer the studio phones, and usher journalists in through the front door. It was so funny; he kept saying 'Who are you again?'

The fourth day arrived and I was whisked off to Radio W.M to do a live interview on air, and Dave was doing the same on the other side of the city over at BRMB radio. Then I was called to BRMB too, to record a piece for the following days breakfast show. In-between all this mayhem we were supposed to be recording the single; we did finish it, but in retrospect I realise it was somewhat rushed with all the press activity going on at the same time.

The following week, if anything, we were more in demand than ever; interviews were recorded for Beacon Radio in Wolverhampton and Dave and I appeared on Radio One's Newsbeat. National tabloid newspaper 'The Sun' sent a photographer round to Dave's house and had us posing in his Dad's garden, and then syndicated the story around the other national press; we appeared in the Daily Mail, Daily Express, The Sun, Daily Mirror, and even The Times and The Guardian. Dave and Martin both went out and got identical tattoos of the first few notes of 'Stop Don't Feel' inked into their upper arms.

Then just as we thought that the publicity was over, we got a call from Central Television wanting us come to the recording studio to record a feature for their early evening news programme. We were going to be on the telly at last! They sent local celebrity Bob Warman down to interview us and let us use the music from our single to promote the record. The same happened the next day with the BBC Midlands Today news programme, and they somehow persuaded Solihull Job Centre to close for an hour to let us film in there, with the bemused Jobseekers looking in from outside.

We felt like stars as the programmes went out, my mum, dad, and sister couldn't believe it; we had only been on the

293

scheme a week and now we were on T.V and Radio. Of course all my aunts, uncles and cousins called up saying they had seen us on the news, it was an amazing feeling. It didn't end there either, before we knew it we were recording a piece for the national Breakfast T.V show hosted by Selina Scott, with Bill Buckley (he of the 'That's Life' TV show fame) interviewing us.

We were then asked to go personally to Number Ten, Downing Street, to present a copy of the record to Margaret Thatcher, the Prime Minister, although at this stage it hadn't yet been pressed, so a cassette would have to suffice. The idea was obviously dreamed up by some spin doctor to make her look like she was down with the kids! We thought it would be fun and we were given a Police escort to the door, while a pack of photographers and foreign tourists took pictures of us from behind steel barriers. We felt like the Beatles! We knocked the door and guess what? Maggie wasn't in, or at least she wasn't coming out to meet us, one of her aides took the tape and letter and closed the door. Our five minutes of fame were up. It did go out on the evening broadcast of News at 5.45, but, we had to watch it silently through a window of a London television store. That night we all slept in the van in an underground car park near Charing Cross Railway Station, much the worse for wear, only to have the BBC send a limousine to pick us up to take us to Lime Grove Studio's the next morning for another interview and to give us a copy of the Breakfast Time broadcast. On our return to Birmingham we were amazed to see local news stands with posters proclaiming "Solihull band in at number ten".

The following week it was the turn of the music press, with small feature mentions in both 'Sounds' and 'Record Mirror' as well as London's 'Time Out' listings magazine.

In September and October we did yet more radio interviews including an hour long phone in show with Robin Valk on BRMB Radio in Birmingham. Safari Records even rang us to ask to hear our demo tapes, so that was another trip to London we had to arrange. I even remember that we rang up Russell Harty to try to get on his chat show; needless to say we got a polite rejection letter through the post.

On October 6th we played another gig at the 'Duma Express Club' in Birmingham and filmed the show for a live video. Being our first home town show since all the T.V exposure, it was a big gig for us and was packed out with reporters and press. It was a really good show and my sister Sue came up and sang backing vocals on a couple of songs too. The reviews were, on the whole, very good and we felt relieved that in our own little way, we had lived up to the previous hype.

Having left the studio during all this activity, with two finished masters, we were still trying to find a permanent keyboard player and had heard on the local grapevine that 'Me-I-Mafia', the band The Undertakers had become, had split up, which meant that Rod Walker their singer and keyboard player was suddenly available. I rang their ex guitarist Paul Hughes to ask for Rod's phone number and by the end of the call he had convinced me to let him join too.

Sarah was happy to let Rod handle backing vocals and split some of the lead vocals too. Therefore we now became a six piece with Sarah (Red) on vocals, Paul Panic on bass, Paul Hughes on Guitar, Dave Browne on second Guitar, Martin hope on Drums and Rod Walker on Keyboards and backing vocals.

The record should have been in the shops to take advantage of all the publicity the band was receiving, but because it had taken us totally by surprise, we were in the frustrating position of being on national television with no product in the shops for people to buy. Then it was decided that a new song Rod and Paul had brought with them from Me-I-Mafia called 'I Lost My Mind' would be a much stronger 'A' side. We booked the Attic Studio's to try it out and then recorded the master at a residential 24 Track studio in Claverdon, Warwickshire called The Barn.

The single was eventually released six months later on February 9th 1984, a date chosen to coincide with our next television appearance, Sarah's sister Carole had done an excellent job on the picture sleeve, but we had mistakenly forgot to put the catalogue number on the sleeve, which resulted in a memorable day at the Nine Mile distribution warehouse in Leamington Spa, applying tiny catalogue number stickers to the backs of hundreds of records, whilst listening to the first Billy Bragg album, 'Life's a riot with spy Vs spy', I seem to remember!

The next bit of good fortune was that, out of the blue, Central Television called us up to invite the band to appear on a show about the 'Enterprise Allowance Scheme', called 'Venture'. The show was actually a business programme but was to be networked across the entire country. The programme featured various businesses that had been set up using the 'Scheme' to establish themselves, such diverse ideas as tattooing and dog grooming and various fashion designers. They asked us to play in the television studios, miming to our single with added live vocals. Then a research assistant mentioned they needed some suitable background music for a section in the programme where they were inserting a pre-recorded film about the other various businesses.

Of course we offered our services, and Central Television financed us, to record a piece of music we had specially written entitled 'Just Want to Do' (what I enjoy and make a life of it). We filmed the show at Central Studio's in Birmingham on February 1st 1984, just prior to the release date of the single, which was now 'I Lost My Mind' with 'Hold Back' on the flipside.

The show was broadcast on February 6th with Eye Do It, playing at the beginning and a full version of the single at the end of the show and our background music behind the middle section. It was also previewed on that evenings Central News show. The show was a big success and got repeated on April 26th, which was good for us as we received a repeat fee as well as a Musician's Union standard fee. That in itself was quite funny as we all had to frantically join the Musician's Union the week before the recording in order to get paid and when we arrived at the television studio's they wouldn't even let us carry our own equipment into the building or change a fuse, without the intervention of a trained union member. You couldn't say 'No' in those days or it would be "Down tools, and all out brothers!"

Local radio picked up the single and gave it some airplay, although Radio W.M in their wisdom played it on Feb 14th, Valentine's Day, at the wrong speed, 33rpm instead of 45rpm, we wrongly assumed D.J's would know about these things.

In the initial publicity, Martin rarely got a mention and no one wanted to interview him as he was the only band member not to be on the 'Enterprise Allowance Scheme', simply because he already had a day job working in a clothing store. It didn't help either that during the first wave of T.V. exposure; he was suffering from a bad case of glandular fever and had completely lost his voice. Shortly after the 'Venture' appearance he decided to leave the band to concentrate on his conventional career. We were really shocked. Me-I-Mafia's ex drummer Dean Marshall (Mario) joined and added a solid back beat which really cemented the band's sound together.

Sarah and I flew to the Spanish island of Majorca to promote the single on May 16th, well o.k., actually we just went on holiday but we managed to get a local nightclub 'Snoopy's' to play the record a few times, it was all good fun. Meanwhile back at home we had become involved with a management company called 'Dreamstar' who paid for professional photo's to be taken of us and arranged a showcase gig for the band at a pub called The Elms in Aldridge on August 2nd 1984, to decide if they wanted to sign us. The gig was good but poorly attended, being out of our local area, and they declined to work with us further.

Then yet another call came in from Central Television reminding us that it was now a year since we had started on the Enterprise Allowance Scheme, and wanting us to record a piece about our success and failures.

On August 14th we were back on the evening news show, explaining that although we would soon be back on the dole, actually the band was musically stronger than ever! The short feature was filmed outside Flick International Recording studios, where we now had our office, and featured Rod, Sarah and myself, giving, a short interview on the future of the band. It was a typical media put down, with quite a few barbed questions.

BBC Radio One soon followed it with an interview with Sarah on 'Newsbeat', where she tried desperately to defend the band. Solihull News also ran an article that week on the band and the end of the grant.

The following evening we played a packed gig at Peacocks bar in Birmingham to the faithful, and I was approached by Sean Purcell from Cuddly Toys after the show, asking me to join them, I think he was impressed by my Japanese kimono! This of course was a huge dilemma at the time for me as they were a big band who I greatly admired. I did go to a few rehearsals with them but it wasn't to be.

We carried on and around this time did more radio interviews for Radio W.M , Beacon Radio, BRMB and others but all they seemed to want to talk about was the apparently failure of the scheme. We figured we had to go out and prove ourselves in a live setting and embarked on a series of gigs, hastily putting together a short tour. We played The Junction in Harbourne, September 1st, Beagles in Acocks Green, September 3rd, Nottingham Vino's, October 23rd, Weymouth Verdi's November 10th, and Birmingham Barrel Organ November 21st.

When we had first started on the scheme the engineer from Attic Studio's, Jon Buxton, with two partners Terry Boazman and Steve Law had moved into a new rehearsal and recording studio complex in Birmingham's Jewellery quarter. It was called Flick International Ltd

It was an underground facility with an 8 Track recording studio and various rehearsal and lock up rooms for bands to hire. We had our own office down there and it was a great way to meet other local bands, as well as some famous names too such as Brian Connolly's Sweet, Felt, and of course, Cuddly Toy's.

The gig we had recently played in Weymouth was at a club called Verdi's, it was a brilliant place to play, and was always packed full right to the back of the venue. It was in an underground cellar bar and it seemed like all of Weymouth's youth would arrive to take advantage of the late bar and of course the great live bands that legendary local promoter Mike Shultz would book. The bands would go on around midnight and always get a lively reaction from the intoxicated crowd. We played there again on January 11th 1985 after being invited back and again later that year on September 5th. Before that happened though, back at Flick Studio's, first Mario and then Rod left the band, I think they both were disillusioned at the band's lack of success, the single had failed to sell in any significant quantities and Rod was keen to try his hand writing a solo project to be called 'The Epic', as well as helping out local reggae band The Cushites with his keyboard skills. We drafted in Terry Boazman (ex Misspent youth) from 'Flick' on Drums and carried on regardless.

We recruited a new keyboard player namely, Mark Burgess, recommended by Terry, who added a new depth of synthesiser skills to the bands mix and he became a full time member on January 25th 1985. Mark brought a new sense of fun and enjoyment to the band, much needed at the time, and constantly entertained us with his many humorous stories and zest for life; he was just the spark we all needed to continue. From then onwards we never needed a diary, Mark had a photographic memory for dates and times. He still is a walking time machine of archival knowledge.

Flick Studio's main man Jon Buxton impressed with the talent of the bands he was hearing through the rehearsal room walls, decided to record a compilation album. I agreed to release it on my label 'No Rip off Records' and Jon spent January and February of '85 recording the sixteen bands that would make up the 'A Night at The Flick's' album. The bands would cover all styles of music from punk to reggae and most styles in-between and the result was a time capsule of what was happening on the Birmingham music scene in 1985.

Eye Do It recorded a new song we had written about the need for the demolition of the Berlin wall entitled 'The Brick Wall' (Knock it Down). It had Terry Boazman on drums, but he was only helping us out, we needed a new sticks man and quick! Mark said he knew a friend who would be 'just the man' and in came Nigel Butcher, who fitted in just fine. Another chapter in the story began. Sarah meanwhile just prior to the recording had briefly left the band and the initial sessions featured a dual vocal of me and my sister Susan. However Sarah soon returned to the band and the vocals were re-recorded to create the version that appears on the released album.

On June 22nd 1985 an open air all day gig was arranged with ten bands from the album playing in the roman style outdoor amphitheatre at Birmingham's Cannon Hill Park. Rod came back and did a guest appearance when we played our single and my sister Sue again returned to provide some backing vocals. It was a triumphant gig for all the bands, unfortunately let down by the unseasonal British summer rain.

We carried on recording new songs at various studios and went to Fallowfield in Manchester on July 21st to film a promotional video for some new songs we had recently recorded at Rich Bitch Studio's, after answering an advert in the music press looking for bands to play at universities. This was a bit of a scam, as on arriving we found around another ten bands all being charged a fee. We quickly worked out that it was a lucrative way for the company to make money with probably no intention of getting the bands the promised gigs. However the resultant video was actually quite well filmed and featured three of our new songs, 'Flames of red', 'Queen of broken hearts' and 'Remember him'.

On July 27th we attended a party at the Outrigger pub in Birmingham headlined by local band Red Shoes and featuring a solo performance by Undertakers bass player Mike Hogan, and were invited onstage to play one song 'Queen of Broken Hearts'. The following day, Nigel left to go on holiday to Singapore, which again put the band on hold for a while. The gigs continued in September with a return to Verdi's in Weymouth on the 5th, this time taking another of the Flick album bands with us - 'Beneath The Street', we had previously taken the gloriously named 'Mangy Bananas'. This was another packed out club night, and another fun performance from us. Dave Browne our roadie who by now we had affectionately rechristened 'Braman' after the chess playing robot in a 1965 episode of 'Thunderbirds', was let loose on the smoke machine and preceded to fill the whole club up with smoke. Dave who originally had worked with The Undertakers (and not to be confused with guitarist Dave, who has the same name) was now helping us out whenever we played, he liked a drink and was often prone to over excitement, I remember the command 'I think that's enough smoke Dave' being shouted rather loudly across the crowd that night!, Oh what fun!

Sadly Dave was due to attend a job interview some years later, but was found dead in his flat in somewhat mysterious circumstances, he will forever be remembered and always be spoken about in very affectionate terms by us all as he was an integral part of all the groups he worked with, as well as a very good friend.

Once again we got invited back to play on our own on November 8th, Unfortunately during the day, Paul Hughes had driven our hire van into club owner Mike's newly erected venue awning; we got banned from returning after that little mishap, especially after Mark then broke a dressing room door.

Two days later we were back in Birmingham and headlining a show at the Railway rock pub in Curzon Street, which was always a good gig, we were due to play again with Beneath The Street, this time the idea was to support them, but their singer, Fiona had lost her voice and we found ourselves headlining once more.

For quite a while we had realised that to get any further in the progression of the bands career we needed to start playing regularly in London, and so we secured a gig at Covent Garden's famous club The Rock Garden as support to a new up and coming band The Doctors Children, who had just released their first single. We really pushed the boat out this time and hired a fifty seat coach, with the idea of selling tickets, transport included, to take down the Birmingham fans of the band.

When the gig arrived on December 4th, we had only sold a handful of tickets to some of the 'Flick' regulars and we ended up incurring a huge loss on costs, but on the plus side we got to travel in style. The resultant gig was played well but didn't create the publicity in the capital we had hoped for. We quickly arranged another one in London the following week on the 12th December at New Merlin's Cave in Kings Cross, with two other bands, Strumpet City, and Sub Rosa, but the first one pulled out at the last minute and the second had an accident on the motorway, which just left us alone to play to the faithful few who bothered to turn up, it was only later we realised the place was usually used as a strip club and they had probably expected a stripper.....

The final gig in 1985 was intended to be a Christmas Eve special show, back at the Railway Rock pub, supporting Atlantic Run who had previously been called The Biz and had also featured on the 'A Night at the Flick's' album. The first support band, whose name now escapes me went on and somehow blew up the P.A system which left the rest of us unable to play, which in turn meant most of the crowd disappeared to look for fun elsewhere. We were left with very little tidings of joy, as we ferried all the equipment back across the city in taxi's to Flick Studio's, thoroughly downhearted. What an end to the year.

As 1986 began we had numerous band meetings to try and find a direction and decided to start a band fund to save up to buy ourselves onto an established tour as a support act. It seemed to us that this was the only way we could finally break out of Birmingham and to play to some large crowds. Sarah's song writing was going from strength to strength and some fine new material was taking shape, songs such as 'San Antonio' and 'Des Camisados' taking the band into new areas of technical perfection. Also unexpectedly,

Central Television ran another feature on the Manpower Services Commission on January 15th and again used our song 'Just wanna do' as backing music to the piece.

We re-entered Rich Bitch Studio's in Selly oak, on February 2nd to demo the new songs, 'San Antonio', 'Des Camisados' and 'Jack of Diamonds' and set up some local radio interviews to preview the songs. In March we printed some band T.shirts which sold well and decided to enter the Battle of the Bands competition to be held at the Dome Nightclub in Birmingham. We were totally against these types of contests but just really wanted to play at this newly opened venue. We played three songs including another new one 'Black Cats' in the regional heats on May 5th. Although we gave our best, the spirit was beginning to fade within the band and the next gig proved to be our last. This was on May 13th 1986 at Maximillions Nightclub in Birmingham. Sarah got very drunk and there was an 'in' band argument about loyalty and lack of commitment by certain members and the ubiquitous musical differences. To be honest I can't even remember how the show went, just a vague memory of bad blood and arguments that marred the evening's performance.

Still we soldiered on for a while longer, first by sacking Nigel as drummer from the band for always being late, and replacing him with a girl drummer from Tamworth called Vicki who had previously played in an early line up of the rock band Wolfsbane. We all went back into Rich Bitch to finish off the previous recordings, and got carried away with numerous over dubs and re mixes. However in the end the recordings stand up as the most accomplished we achieved in the bands career. Vicki then quit the band and we became drummer less once more.

Felt, fronted by the enigmatic 'Lawrence' were another band using 'Flick' Studio's at this time, and had been recording their fifth album, 'Let the snakes crinkle their heads to death' for Creation Records there, engineered by Jon Buxton. Lawrence had listened to one of our rehearsals and invited Sarah to sing backing vocals on their forthcoming single 'Rain of Crystal Spires', which they recorded at Leamington's Woodbine St Studio's. Sarah and I accompanied the band to Leamington Spa, and Lawrence was so impressed by the Public Image Ltd shirt I was wearing that he actually bought it off my back. Sarah can be heard on the single release and does a great job although on the day I think she was a little overwhelmed by the fact that Liz Fraser from the Cocteau Twins had previously performed backing vocal duties on another of Felt's songs. The other major happening in 1986 was that I moved out into my own flat, as my parents decided to move to Spain to retire to the sun, my sister eventually moved to London to work at Harrods. It was time to grow up, I guess.

By late '86 the remnants of the band had moved from 'Flick' to rehearse at a new Studio rehearsal complex in Birmingham called 'Fastix'. We were discussing new recordings after Christmas but another disagreement over direction arose and resulted in guitarist Paul Hughes walking out on the band. We had all been saving hard, even buying and selling shares in British Gas as I recall, with the idea of buying onto a tour as support to a well known band. There was also talk of American dates, as one of Fastix's owners Stuart was American and said he could arrange a small tour. The problems arose when it came to actually giving up day jobs, Mark had actually handed in his notice but Paul Hughes was a little more wary and this led to a few heated discussions between them. Paul and Mark had a disagreement one day about Paul being late for a session and he promptly walked out never to return. After that blow, we simply lost heart and split the band up for good, this was January 1987. Sarah and I, and a long term friend of the band Andy Foxall went into the 'Barn' studio to record some new demo's but by this time mine and Sarah's personal relationship was on rocky ground too. I eventually left them to it. Paul Hughes and keyboards player Mark Burgess despite their differences, also recorded demo's

311

together but nothing solid emerged. We were all still in touch but time had moved on and no more music was forthcoming.

Rich Bitch Studio's in Selly Oak, Birmingham, used to hold music business seminars to teach local musicians about the mechanics and evil ways of the music industry. It was actually really interesting to hear other people's tales of woe, and occasional success too. Local luminaries would be on the panel ranging from music business lawyers to Jo Dunne from 'Fuzzbox' or Rob Lloyd from the Nightingales/Vindaloo Records, all telling their musical tales.

At one of these meetings I met a guy called Billy Nash who needed a bass player for a new project. Billy, I think, saw himself as a kind of an Asian Elvis Presley, but interestingly combined some hints of Bhangra music into his songs too. I agreed to play bass, and our keyboard player from Eye Do It, Mark Burgess was brought into the band too, simply called the Billy Nash Band. The guitarist was a friend of Billy's called Mark Jago and his sister Shirene and friend Helen Pritchett were the backing vocalists and dancers. The line up was completed by another girl called Sandra Sterling on percussion. We rehearsed and played some shows in London during 1988 at

'La Vie En Rose' Club and the 'Break for the Border' venues, as well as recording a video at the 'Pagoda Park' nightclub in Birmingham and performing at the club on the evening. Billy arranged some promotional gigs where we simply turned up and mimed to backing tracks during weekend club nights at various venues, I particularly remember playing to a packed house of bemused revellers in one such club in Worcester, another one somewhere in Hereford, as well as a performance at a large Bhangra all day event at the Hummingbird Club in Birmingham. Fun while it lasted, but eventually various members left and it was left to Billy and I to record a new Bhangra hip hop track at UB40's 'Abattoir Studio's', for possible single release, which led to a video promo being made to promote it, with the help of another new girl member called 'Alex'. It was fun while it lasted but eventually I left the band.

I continued with music of course, and by 1989 had got a job at the Birmingham 'Virgin Megastore', which was to last for the next fifteen years. Sarah and I sadly split up a few years after I had moved out of the family home; we had been together around six years, had a lot of fun but, maybe being in a band with your girlfriend was never a good idea.

In March 1990 I became bass guitarist with a band called The Press Darlings, which was formed with two colleagues

313

from my workplace at Virgin; John Hassell on guitar and Sandra O'Reilly on vocals. We had gone to see the band Lush perform at Burberries Club in Broad Street, Birmingham, and decided there and then to form a band of our own. After trying out our ex 'Accused' drummer Simon Baker, we settled on another work colleague, Richard Wise as the sticks man. It was only to be the occupant of the drum stool that would change over the next couple of years, as we went on to record demo's, play gigs both locally and also in such diverse locations as Belfast, Stourbridge, Bridgewater, and the Channel island of Guernsey, the later booked by our drummer at the time Shaun Broughton. Shaun was a Guernsey resident himself but at the time was in Birmingham working with us at Virgin. I eventually left the band about three years later but they went on to release one C.D. single and had many line up changes, playing around locally and in London and also touring Germany a couple of times. At the time of writing there is a retrospective album of previously unissued material due.

With the advent of the internet I started getting many enquiries from punk collectors around the world, mainly about The Accused and my label No Rip off Records. Martin and I discussed reforming the band and eventually a new line up was put together adding Kevin (chex) Checkley on lead vocals and Richard Wise on drums , I was to play bass and Martin Hope(less), guitar. We also later added a second guitarist Dee Smith to play his own style of manic lead guitar (a true star!). The idea was that I would share some of the lead vocals with Kevin, but we wanted to avoid a simple retread of the original band and soon after changed the name of the band to Bride Just Died, after one of The Accused' earliest songs.

We started off playing all The Accused' old songs but soon added new compositions too. We played a number of gigs in and around Birmingham and recorded eleven songs at 'De Havilland' studios in Tamworth in 1994. It was a return to playing fast punk, the difference being that this time around we could actually play tightly together as a band, Richard being a powerhouse drummer and Kevin being a very strong front man. Martin and I however eventually decided to leave it to the younger members. The band went on after our departure to greater things. They released a red vinyl seven inch single and got a deal with N.D.M Records in the United States and recorded an album, 'All Hallows Eve' with none other than the legendary Damned drummer, Rat Scabies in the producer's chair.

The last band of any significance that I joined was Heronimus Fin, a magnificent Psychedelic outfit fronted by my old friend Jon Buxton (George) from Flick International

315

Studios who was in one of Birmingham's first punk bands Misspent Youth and had released a single on Big Bear Records in 1979 called 'Betcha won't Dance/Birmingham Boys'.

The four piece line up was completed by Jeremy the Cat on Keyboards and Mike (Mik) on drums, the band released three albums, 'The World according to Heronimus Fin' (1995), 'Riding the Great Fantastic' (1998) and 'Bloodguilt' (2001) on the indie label Garden Records. We actually recorded a final fourth album called 'Beat the Cistern' which in my opinion contains some of the bands finest work, but sadly at the time of writing remains un-released. A C.D. single was released called the Purple Pictures E.P. and there was also the recording and release of the C.D. single of 'Animal Tragic' (Who are the real animals anyway?) a benefit/protest single highlighting the sad fate of Trudy the chimp allegedly abused by circus trainer Mary Chipperfield. The time was now 1999 and the court case, resulted in a cameo appearance by members of the band and our audio/visual expert Ian Edwards dressed up in a monkey suit, joining in with the protests outside the court in Aldershot.

We went to visit Trudy the chimpanzee at the Monkey world sanctuary in Dorset and made all the local papers.

Before we knew it we were on Breakfast Television promoting the single and even made a memorable appearance on our own half hour slot on the Ideal World Shopping channel. I bet no other Psychedelic band has ever achieved that, it was the absolute pinnacle of surrealism, helped somewhat by the contents of the green room's fridge! Gigs were carefully chosen to preserve the mystery of the band, but we did play in Camden Town at 'The Laurel Tree', as well as supporting ex Family man, Roger Chapman at the famous London Astoria venue.

The band's other interesting fact is that for many years we were in the world's most collectable 500 bands chart in Record Collector magazine, eclipsing many household names, unbelievable but true! In 2002 we came in at number 247 above the MC5, Robert Plant and Foo Fighters, to name just three.

Each of the four band member's of Heronimus Fin recorded solo projects and mine was named Apple Overground, releasing 2 songs recorded in a studio in Hull ('Paradise Universe' and 'A world and its component parts'), recorded with the help of girlfriend at the time, Sharon Reilly on Vocals on the first track. The tracks were subsequently released on the Garden Records Sampler C.D. I then drafted in Press Darlings guitarist John Hassell and Bride Just Died drummer Richard Wise to record some more as yet unissued demo's at the Garden Records recording facility in Droitwich, Worcestershire.

The Mell Square Musick EP these days is a worldwide collector's item amongst punk music fans, and has led to the release of the four original band's demo's on a double C.D. release issued on the 'Only Fit for the Bin' records label, 'Mell Square Musick–The Album' courtesy of Dizzy Holmes from Detour Records. It also prompted me to film and release a feature length movie DVD telling the story of the E.P and the punk scene back in 1970's Birmingham and Solihull, that is called Mell Square Musick–The Movie'.

The interest in our little homemade record never seems to end; people all over the world still contact me via the internet regularly asking the most obscure questions. The Accused re-union demo's have also now been given an official release on Sheffield label Retro Records under the title 'The Accused - Standing Trial', and at last 'A Tale of Two Cities' the Compilation album I compiled back in 1981 with Lorraine Adey, and 'A Night at the Flicks' have both now been released on CD, again via Retro Records.

As for me I remain as ever involved in music. Without music in my life I don't think I would be able to function, it is there both for the good times and the bad. It can lift the spirits during the dark times and both cleanse the soul and calm the emotions. These days it is necessary to search and dig deeper than in days gone by for the real talent, as once again the charts have become bland and boring, reflecting the throwaway world we now all have to live within. A good catchy tune lasts a month but a real melody lasts forever, and don't even get me started on the TV talent shows!!

I continue to search for real happiness in life, these days occasionally battling anxiety and the loss of people who were close to me, both alive and dead. A smile can mask your real self, but if you give out your love, hopefully you may get some back in return. But I guess as Jimmy Pursey said all those years ago and Frank Sinatra before him in my parent's day 'That's Life'

THE END

OR, IS IT JUST THE BEGINNING?

DISCOGRAPHY

7" SINGLE RELEASES

The Accused

Generation Gap- Track on Mell Square Musick E.P. 1979

Solihull- Track on Mell Square Musick E.P. 1979

Arrested- Track on Mell Square Musick E.P. 1979

Cracked Actors

Disco – Track on Mell square Musick E.P 1979

Statues / On the line- self released by band in 1980

Rock 'n' roll Fantasy / Calling for Time -self released by band in 1980

O21

Robot (Don't wanna be a) – Track on Mell Square Musick E.P. 1979

Simple Minds/Whatever Happened to You

20 copies Test Pressings only 1980 White Labels

The Pop Song/Aversion- U.K. Pop Records 1982

The Undertakers

Illusions- Track on Mell Square Musick E.P. 1979

Mell Square Musick E.P. Catalogue Number: No Rip off Records Yaw 001

Eye Do It

I Lost My Mind/Hold Back- No Rip off Records 1984 Yaw 002

Bride Just Died

We Are the Hungry/House That Bleeds/All Hallows Eve/Norman Bates NDN Records 1998 NDN14 1st 100 Copies Silk Screen Art cover, 900 copies Diff Sleeve, all Red Vinyl

Misspent Youth

Betcha Won't Dance/Birmingham Boys

Big Bear Records BB20 1979

ALBUM RELEASES

Mell Square Musick – The Album Only Fit for the Bin Records 2010- Double C.D. cat number OFFTB007, unreleased tracks from:

The Accused:

Solihull revisited/Police State (live)/Photo Copy Views/Bride Just Died/She'd Gone Punk/Hellhole/W.M.P.T.E./Don't Wanna Be In 021/London/We're Crap

Cracked Actors:

Disco/Statues/Calling for Time/Rock'N'Roll Fantasy/Subway/On the Line

021: The Pop Song/Aversion (Demo) /Class of '78/Secret Lover/Hitting Town Tonite/Words to the Wise

The Undertakers: I Just Wanna (Make Love To you)/Monotony/Sadistic Lady/Overload/English Nation/Three Coffins in My Head

A Night at The Flicks – The Birmingham Compilation L.P.

No Rip off Records 1985 YAW 003 Vinyl 16 Tracks

Features:

Eye Do It – The Brick Wall (Knock it Down)

King Rat – That's Progress

Now also available on C.D. on Retro Records 2015

A Tale Of Two Cities – Birmingham and Coventry 1981 No Rip Off Records Initially released on Cassette only 100 copies, but re-released as a 17 track C.D. in 2012 on Retro Records/No Rip Off records RET 16/YAW 004

Features:

The Undertakers – Overload

The Accused – Generation Gap

021 – I Eat Women

The Accused – Standing Trial, The Long Lost tapes

C.D. Album Retro Records/No Rip Off records 2012 RET 11/Yaw 006

11 Studio recorded Tracks.

Features:

Bride Just Died/Nothing Goes Right/Queen Of Broken Hearts/Moseley Punk song/What's It like To be Old?/We're Crap/Middle East Peace/I'm the urban Spaceman/Solihull re-visited/She'd Gone Punk/In a Rut/Rocking In The Free world/Girls At Number 42

Messthetics # 103 D.I.Y Midlands 77-81 HII 2D Compilation C.D. 2007.

Features 26 Tracks Inc

The Accused – Arrested

The Accused – She'd Gone Punk

Cracked Actors – Statues

021 – Robot (Don't wanna be a)

Bloodstains across Birmingham C.D. 2013

Features 28 Tracks Inc

The Accused – Solihull

The Undertakers – Illusions

Cracked Actors – Disco

The Accused- Shirley Temple's Dead C.D.

21 Tracks of early Demo's with previously unreleased songs from 1979 (Retro Records RET 20 2013)

The Accused- Live at the Star Club 1980 C.D.

13 live tracks recorded at Birmingham's Star Club and one previously thought lost, demo.

This CD perfectly captures the early punk spirit of the band and the crowd and includes previously unreleased songs. (Retro Records RET 24 2014)

PowerPoppers Vol 1 Vinyl L.P

Features

021 – The pop Song (On the Run records 2001)

The Garden Records Sampler C.D. Garden Records GCD 004 1998

Features:

Apple Over-ground – Paradise Universe

Apple Over-ground – A World and its Component Parts

Misspent Youth –The Punk Years 1976-1980

10 Track C.D.released by Garden Records GCD008

Released in 2002 C.D only

Bride Just Died – All Hallows Eve C.D. Album
N.D.N Records NDN 25 2000

It's A Damned, Damned, World

NDN Records C.D. NDN12

Features:

Bride Just Died – Suicide

021- All Was Nothing C.D. Album

Paisley Archive Records PA 038 2015

15 Tracks including many previously unreleased.

The Undertakers - Down to Hell . . . . (and back)!!

C.D. Album coming soon.

DVD RELEASES

Mell Square Musick – The Movie Double DVD

No Rip Off YAW 005

A Two Hour Film of the complete story of the 4 bands from the original E.P. includes archive film, interviews, rare footage and photo archive as well as one hour of extra footage on disc 2 available now mellsquaremusick@hotmail.com

Simon Baker still livin' the dream....Movin' on a groove!

(Photo kindly supplied by Ted Dale)

DEMO TAPES APPEAL

If you were in an early Punk/New wave band and still have tapes, no matter how badly recorded, I would love to hear from you, your music deserves to be heard!

Does anyone for example, have recordings of Solihull bands such as?

Life Support /A Mental Block /Mass Media

Please E Mail me, Paul Panic

mellsquaremusick@hotmail.com

Check out the releases from

Retro Records: **http://www.punkdomain.com**

And Detour Records here:

http://www.detour-records.co.uk

AFTERWORD

Here we are some thirty five years on from the release of our little cheaply recorded and glued together masterpiece from the suburbs, now known worldwide as the legendary 'Mell Square Musick E.P.'

Of course to put this in context, it is only known on a worldwide basis, and is only legendary to those in the know and only to those that care in the complex world of Punk Rock record collecting. However who would have thought, and certainly not us, that all these years later, that anyone would care at all about a few musicians (and even that is said loosely, in some cases) from Solihull, who made their own record in 1979. With the advent of the internet the world has become smaller, and people can make contact with each other in just a few clicks. This can be the only explanation, as with every year that passes, I continue to receive E-mails from all around the world asking for information about the record and/or the bands featured on it. It was with this in mind that in 2004 I embarked on another D.I.Y project to address many of the questions people wanted answering. I had no experience at all as a film maker but off I went armed with just a domestic camcorder to try to document the bands story and that of the times, it did cross my mind that actually this is about as Punk Rock, do it yourself, as it gets!. The result some five years later was a 2 hour movie and an hour's worth of extra footage that all ended up on the DVD release 'Mell Square Musick-The Movie'. I spoke to old friends and associates I had not seen for over thirty years and they recounted stories of incidents I had completely forgotten about, and to you all, I would like to say "It was a joy".

One thing that soon became apparent during this process, was that people's memories record events in very different ways; it's just as if the memory creates its own rules that suit each person's mood and of course always in their own favour. With cross examination of the suspects however, the truth was usually established, nearly everyone blamed it on old age approaching! I even managed to reform The Accused for a one off appearance in the film, and we even wrote a new song for the occasion called 'Kill all the Boy Bands'.

Then one day I got the holy grail of offers from Dizzy Holmes at Detour Records – an actual offer of a record deal! Thoughts of The Clash selling out to C.B.S flooded my brain for a second, but Dizzy I knew was a true gent and an industrious searcher out of all things punk and mod and when it became clear that he wanted to give a release to all those demo tapes we had kept in cupboards and lofts un-played for years I readily agreed.

The resultant album included previously unreleased songs from all the bands from the Mell Square Musick E.P. and even a complete broadcast of John Peel playing tracks from it, which pleased me as he was always a big part of our story. It was released as a double C.D., by Dizzy on the affectionately titled 'Only Fit for the Bin' Records label, called 'Mell Square Musick- the Album' and is currently available online.

This book concludes the trilogy of releases (Album, Film, and Book) and again was partly written in response to continuing requests for more information from around the globe. It was also a way of me exorcising my ghosts from the past but again it has brought me in touch with many interesting discoveries from that time, both human and material. Suddenly seeing photographs I never knew existed taken over thirty years ago, and sent to me from Italy from Nick Hartshorn, our borrowed bass player from The Androids, was incredible for example, as were photo's discovered by my friend David Coombs taken at the Band's first gig at Solihull Civic Hall, that I didn't know even existed. When I finally saw these pictures my jaw dropped to the floor, for they showed that we had indeed had a Bass player at that first gig. Here all of a sudden was someone I couldn't identify or even remember playing with us. I immediately contacted the rest of the band and showed them the photos, but to my amazement no one could remember this guy playing with us either. At the time of writing he still hasn't been positively identified, but strangely our guitarist Dave Browne does recognise the T-shirt this person was wearing as a treasured one of his own. All very strange; If you recognise yourself in the Photo please get in touch, you deserve some credit, or you will be forever be remembered as a ghost!

In 2010, I was approached by producers Roger Shannon and Jez Collins, to appear in a film to be made and directed by Deborah Aston via Swish Films in conjunction with the Birmingham Music Archive. The result is a film called 'Made in Birmingham-Reggae, Punk, and Bhangra' which chronicles many early Birmingham bands such as The Prefects, The Killjoys, Denizens, Au Pairs, The Surprises, Spizz, Fuzzbox, as well as The Accused, The Beat, UB40, Steel Pulse, Beshara, Musical Youth, and the Bhangra scene. Highly recommended for the rare early footage it contains. During a preview screening I was approached by Brian Travers from UB40, who actually remembers attending one of The Accused gigs at the Star Club in Birmingham, who would have thought?

And then I got an E-Mail from my ex workmate Polly D'abo via a well known social networking site, asking if I knew that the Mell Square Musick E.P. was being exhibited in an instillation at the Hayward Art Gallery on the South Bank in London.........'Someday all the Adults will Die'..... Curated by Johan Kugelburg and Jon Savage Punk Graphics 1971-1984

Solihull Punks, in an art gallery?

Whoever would have thought it possible?

On November 28th 2010, the Mell Square Musick Album was reviewed as a 'Must have re-issue of the Week' in the Sunday Times Magazine.

And then in the December 2013 edition of Record Collector Magazine, the Mell Square Musick E.P got voted 14th best outsider punk rock record in the world, incredible!

Whatever Next?

There are even plans to get all four bands from the E.P to reform for the book launch, plenty of bald heads to be seen that night, but great that we are all still friends.

Paul Panic 2015

If you wish to contact the author please E-Mail:

mellsquaremusick@hotmail.com

Book cover artwork and design by Jodie Wingham.

jodiewingham@hotmail.com

Back cover photograph of Paul Hughes (The Undertakers), photo by Neil Parker.

Book printed by Catford Print Centre

web@catfordprint.co.uk

CREDITS

I would like to thank the following people for kindly allowing me to reproduce photographs from their personal collections, every effort was made to contact the photographers of the images used in these pages. Thanks to:

Anthony Simpson, Paul Hughes, Rod Walker, Mike Carter, Simon Baker, Nick Hartshorn, Mark Rhodes David Coombs, Neil Parker, Ted Dale.

Thanks also to the following for contributing their own memories in writing:

Jean Debney, Mike Hogan, Roger Springer, Tony Simpson, David Wright, Mike Carter and Max Body

And for help, inspiration, patience, support and friendship:

John Peel, Mum and Dad, Susan Lawson, Martin Hope, Simon Baker, David Browne, Tim (Ed) Eccles, Steve Clarke, Paul Hughes, Mike Hogan, Rod Walker, Dean (Mario)Marshall, Jean Debney, Eileen Coyle, Samantha

Collings, Dave 'Braman' Browne (RIP), Tony Simpson, Martin Frain, Colin Abrahall, David Wright, Julie Marshall, Mike Carter, David White, David Coombs, Polly D'abo, Rob Peters, Sharon Reynolds, Steve Teers, Jon Buxton, Terry Boazman, Mark Burgess, Sarah Winsper, Carole Thompson nee Winsper, Ken Winsper, Nigel Butcher, Dizzy Holmes, Chuck Warner, Paul Kelly, Sean O'Neill, Alex Ogg, Mark Freeth, Glyn 'Taffy' Rickards, Ian Kemp, Ian Richards, Michael Hancox, Jez Collins, Deborah Aston, John Hassell, Phil Lunn, Richard Wise, Kevin Checkley, Pebbles, Joanne Hope, Roger Springer, Keeley Garvie, Mark Rhodes, Paul read, Sue Beattie, Jodie Wingham.

Special thanks to Paul 'Hudges' Hughes for original text/photo layouts and invaluable financial help in bringing this project to print.

And the last word goes to Stewart Lee, renowned comedian who grew up in Solihull, who wrote in a recent review of Mell Square Musick the album;

"..This fascinating snapshot of a regional micro-scene gives evidence of punk's inspirational effect on suburban kids nationwide".

As this picture shows, it sure is fun, being in a band!!?

Mark Burgess (keyboards) and Nigel Butcher (drums) from Eye Do It